Praise for *You and We*

"Some books make you think. This one changes how you see everything. Beautifully written, thought-provoking, and utterly unique—this book could actually change the world."
—Ken Blanchard, Coauthor, *The New One Minute Manager*®
and *Simple Truths of Leadership*

"This book will forever change how you think about life and leadership."
—Adel Al-Saleh, CEO, SES

"*You and We* is a tour de force on the relational nature of reality and what that means for management, politics, and personal relationships. I read it in awe and will no doubt join Jim Ferrell and others in promoting the book's ideas as part of my calling for the rest of my life."
—Avraham (Avi) N. Kluger, Professor of
Organizational Behavior, Hebrew University

"Every so often, a book becomes a mirror and a map—reflecting who we are and showing who we might become. *You and We* is that rare guide. Reading it moved me. Challenged me. Made me wish I'd written it. Don't just read this book. Let it change you. Disruptive. Profound. Practical. Brilliant."
—Whitney Johnson, CEO, Disruption Advisors
and Bestselling Author, *Smart Growth*

"I'm struggling to find words to adequately capture how consequential this book will be for our world. *You and We* is revolutionary. It is the most significant book about human relationships written in the past two decades. At a time when the world is tearing apart, the ideas and principles in this book are the key to solving our most intractable interpersonal, intersocial, and international crises."
—Chad Ford, international Conflict Mediator, and
Author, *Seventy Times Seven* and *Dangerous Love*

"As a founder and leader in quantum computing, I found *You and We* to be a leadership page-turner I couldn't put down! Jim Ferrell has managed to write this profoundly original book on human connection and courageous leadership at a time when the world needs it most. It's rare these days to encounter a completely fresh take on leadership, but this book is exactly that. Entertaining, humbling, and quietly transformative, it left me thinking about life and leadership in ways I never had before."
—Rebecca Krauthamer, CEO, QuSecure

"*You and We* is a game changer. It offers a profound new perspective on relationships that has the power to transform not just our personal lives but our organizations and our world. It helped me adopt a fundamentally new perspective toward relationships beyond anything I have encountered in other books. In a world that often seems torn apart, this book is a powerful reminder of the transformative power of connection and community."

—Philipp Kohler-Redlich, Vice President, Technology, Infineon Technologies

"A book that applies phenomenology and quantum physics to . . . business leadership? And it reads like a work of fiction, with compelling characters you actually believe in and care about? *You and We* is all that and more. Jim Ferrell advances a new vision for making communities, businesses, and even society as a whole work better, more equitably, and for the greater benefit of all. It is a revolutionary achievement."

—William Egginton, Decker Professor in the Humanities,
Johns Hopkins University, author of *The Rigor of Angels: Borges,
Heisenberg, Kant, and the Ultimate Nature of Reality*

"*You and We* is profound, and its ideas have real, practical impact. I know that firsthand, as one of my all-time favorite projects was engaging with Jim Ferrell on an organizational journey to raise our overall company connectivity scores. We successfully drove improvements in relation both within teams and across the organization in dramatic ways within every function and at every level of the company. *You and We* is a page-turning guide on how to apply these powerful principles to every relationship and connection."

—Melissa Knotts, CPO, Vasion, Silicon Slopes
Chief People Officer of the Year

"Profound, captivating, and deeply moving. If you are concerned about the divides threatening society, this book is for you. If you are a leader looking for ways to access the untapped potential of your business, this book is for you. If you are tired of surface-level interactions and want to connect more deeply with others, this book is for you. *You and We* changes you at a personal level while also laying out a powerful blueprint for organizational and societal change. Reading it was a paradigm-shifting experience that gives me both direction and hope."

—John Fikany, CEO, The Fikany Group,
and former Vice President, Microsoft

"*You and We* arrives precisely when we need it most. As society fragments into increasingly hostile camps, Ferrell illuminates the revolutionary truth that our breakthrough lies not in victory over others but in the courage to open ourselves to genuine relation, even across differences. With rare clarity and profound insight, Ferrell shows how the spaces between our differences can become the birthplace of solutions our fractured world desperately needs."

—Joel Dehlin, CEO, Kuali

"In *You and We*, Jim Ferrell presents a groundbreaking exploration of relational leadership, blending profound insights from quantum physics, philosophy, and real-world organizational dynamics. Ferrell reveals that true progress arises not from managing individuals in isolation, but from fostering the dynamic connections that bind us together. It is a must-read for anyone seeking to lead, connect, and thrive in an interconnected world."

—Oliver Herrmann, Head of Employee Wellbeing,
Health, and Safety, Deutsche Telekom

"Jim Ferrell brings vital, transformational, and immediately applicable ideas in a brilliant format that envelops the reader emotionally and intellectually—from the first page of *You and We* to the last. He weaves deep philosophical, psychological, and pragmatic insights into a compelling story that pulls the reader into examining their own relationships, leadership, and life situation. Most importantly, he shows a path for how the reader can become the person they always hoped they would be."

—James Flaherty, MCC, Founder, New Ventures West and Integral Coaching

"Written by one of the premier thought leaders and deep thinkers of this generation, Jim Ferrell unfolds and describes in an easy-to-read story the fundamental principles of relation and how they impact our relationships in any environment or setting. If you want to have your eyes opened and challenge the norms on relationship development and connection with others, *You and We* is a must-read."

—Mark Ferguson, former Director, Employee and Labor Relations, Raytheon

"It's rare to find a business book that makes leadership topics feel this human, this real and personal. It's not about another framework, hack, or quick-fix strategy but about breaking through the stuff that holds us back from truly connecting. This is deep, powerful, and truly transformational work."

—Emanuele Mazzanti, Learning and Development Leader, EY Nordics

"In *You and We*, Jim Ferrell uses his storytelling skills expertly to invite each reader to explore new ways of thinking about leadership and relating to people. Reading *You and We* gave me new and powerful language to describe how I relate to others and the world. Where possible, I recommend that you read the book with others. If you do, its message on relationality will do far more than teach you a new skill; it will help you to discover a superpower."

—Kim Bilyeu, Director, Worldwide Education,
Johnson & Johnson MedTech

"Insightful and refreshingly approachable, *You and We* blends engaging storytelling with profound and practical ideas that skillfully reframe how you lead, live, and engage in deep reflection for personal growth. If you're ready to move beyond the typical leadership checklist and embrace a more vibrant, whole, and connected way of thinking, this is a book you don't want to miss."

—Dr. Chris Dalton, Associate Professor, Henley Business School, UK

"In *You and We*, Jim Ferrell doesn't just offer a framework for leadership; he invites us into a new way of being—one rooted in the undeniable power of relation over individualism. This book has supercharged my commitment to serve humanity with clarity, courage, and connection."

—John Register, Resilience Architect, Professional Speaker, and CEO, Inspired Communications International

"A riveting read that shows what's possible in work, life, and love when you awaken from the sleep of separation to the reality of relation. You will see a different and more hopeful world unfold all around you."

—Bruce A. Berger, PhD, Emeritus Professor, Auburn University

"*You and We* gives me hope. It is fun and engaging, deep and profound. I see myself and the role I play in my life differently having read it. Any organization that took this on would make a giant leap forward."

—Suzanne Thomas, Executive Coach and former Vice President, Digital, Marriott International

"*You and We* addresses the fabric of existence and relationships in such a simple and beautiful way that I can see immediate application to my life and business. Seeing and appreciating the uniqueness of others as a way to build something great together takes the mental blockers off and allows for a new creation to begin."

—Jacob Baadsgaard, Founder and CEO, Disruptive Advertising

"*You and We* is a transformational read that pressed right up against some of my core beliefs and challenged me to rethink how I approach every interaction. It's rare that a book reframes and reshapes one's perspectives, and I highly recommend this remarkable work to anyone who wants to experience meaningful growth and connection."

—Philip Russo, Global Chief Design and Innovation Officer, Vans

YOU AND WE

A Relational Rethinking of
Work, Life, and Leadership

YOU AND WE

JIM FERRELL

Matt Holt Books
An Imprint of BenBella Books, Inc.
Dallas, TX

This book is designed to provide accurate and authoritative information about personal and professional development. Neither the author nor the publisher is engaged in rendering legal, accounting, or other professional services by publishing this book. If any such assistance is required, the services of qualified professionals should be sought. The author and publisher will not be responsible for any liability, loss, or risk incurred as a result of the use and application of any information contained in this book.

You and We copyright © 2025 by James Ferrell

All rights reserved. Except in the case of brief quotations embodied in critical articles or reviews, no part of this book may be used or reproduced, stored, transmitted, or used in any manner whatsoever, including for training artificial intelligence (AI) technologies or for automated text and data mining, without prior written permission from the publisher.

Matt Holt is an imprint of BenBella Books, Inc.
8080 N. Central Expressway
Suite 1700
Dallas, TX 75206
benbellabooks.com
Send feedback to feedback@benbellabooks.com

BenBella and *Matt Holt* are federally registered trademarks.

Printed in the United States of America
10 9 8 7 6 5 4 3 2 1

Library of Congress Control Number: 2025010120
ISBN 978-1-63774-733-9 (hardcover)
ISBN 978-1-63774-734-6 (electronic)

Copyediting by Michael Fedison
Proofreading by Cheryl Beacham and Becky Maines
Indexing by Debra Bowman
Text design and composition by PerfecType, Nashville, TN
Cover design by Brigid Pearson
Printed by Versa Press

Special discounts for bulk sales are available. Please contact bulkorders@benbellabooks.com.

*To all who are open to seeing reality as they've
never seen it before. And to my partner, Kathrin, with whom a
relational understanding of work, life, and leadership
has become powerfully obvious.*

CONTENTS

Preface xv

PART I A New Paradigm

1 The Chosen 3

2 Questions 11

3 Surprises 17

4 The Only Thing We See 27

5 The *We* Called *Me* 35

6 Intersecting into Being 41

7 Making Water 45

PART II Thinking Relationally

8 Levels of Relation 53

9 Relational Maps 63

10 The 4-Dimensional Playing Field 77

11 Divides and Differences 89

12 Hegel's Spiral 97

13 Breaking, Blocking, Bonding, and Bridging 105

14 Putting It Together 117

PART III Expanding

15 Ruminations 125

16 Trapped in Our Heads 131

17 Buber's Hyphen 141

18 Breaking Open 151

19 Connecting 161

20 Differences Coming Together 171

21 Offering Your *Du* 179

PART IV The Relational Leap

22 Alone 189

23 Wholes or Parts 193

24 Another Chance 201

25 Together Differently 211

26 A New Beginning 223

Epilogue 227

Acknowledgments 229

Notes 231

Index 237

About the Author 245

What's Next 246

"In the beginning is relation."
—Martin Buber[1]

"It is only in interactions that
nature draws the world."
—Carlo Rovelli[2]

"We can progress only by uniting:
this is the law of life."
—Pierre Teilhard de Chardin[3]

PREFACE

Progress requires a willingness to open ourselves to new ideas, as well as the courage to let go of old concepts that used to serve us well. It demands that we question the status quo.

I was perfectly comfortable with my status quo when I boarded a flight to Germany several years ago. I had packed two books by the philosopher Martin Buber, who had long been an intellectual hero of mine. His ideas had been among the key inspirations for my work with leaders and organizations around the world over the prior decades, and I was excited for the uninterrupted time to read and study him again.

I started into the first of the books just after takeoff. Somewhere over the Atlantic, however, a passage he wrote stopped me short. I put the book down and closed my eyes. I had to find my bearings. What I had just read suggested that much of what I thought I knew about Buber and his work was mistaken. I had read him too thinly, too naively, too quickly. He was making a far deeper and more fundamental point than I had ever before understood, with a host of astonishing implications.

This wasn't a small matter, because it meant that I may have unwittingly spread a misunderstanding to tens of thousands of people in speeches and workshops I had delivered, not to mention the millions of people who had read earlier books I had written. What I had shared both in person and in writing all those years wasn't inherently wrong, and in many situations was still immensely helpful, both to others and myself. But it was also incomplete in ways that I didn't begin to realize until that eureka moment on the plane.

At the time, I had recently retired from the Arbinger Institute, a leadership training and consulting firm I led for over two decades. I ended up at Arbinger through a combination of fate and chance. I had graduated from Yale Law School and was practicing law at one of the country's mega-firms when I crossed paths with a philosophy professor with whom I had studied during my undergraduate years. I revered him and his work, and within a year that reconnection caused me to leave the practice of law and join him and a few others in the project of bringing his then new and fascinating body of work to the world.

Over the years at Arbinger, I threw myself into the study of inter-human connection, which is when I first encountered Buber's work. I started boiling down very complex but important ideas into concepts, diagrams, and other digestible forms that would lend themselves to easy practical application. During these developmental times, I also wrote the original versions of Arbinger's bestselling books, *Leadership and Self-Deception* and *The Anatomy of Peace*.[4] These books have been translated into more than 30 languages and have sold many millions of copies. Their success has put me in boardrooms and on convention stages all around the world. But on that flight to Germany, I realized that, for decades, despite the best of intentions, I had been blocked from helping people more powerfully because there was something fundamental, right under my nose, that I had been missing.

So began, for me, a new and far deeper interdisciplinary exploration into the emerging understanding of the world of *relation*. When I say *relation*, I'm not talking about relationships. I'm referring, instead, to our fundamental connectedness—to how the worlds of work and home and leadership, as well as the worlds within ourselves, are constructed by our intersections.

PREFACE   xvii

What do I mean by that? Consider the example of this book. As I write these words, I am thinking of you, the reader—imagining who you are, what kinds of words and explanations would be helpful to you, what kinds of challenges or interests have caused you to crack open this book, and what my wish for you in encountering it would be. In that respect, *your* presence for me is pressing the keyboard as much as my fingers are! I am also driven and influenced by all the conversations I have had with those around me, by the work of other thinkers I have been in conversation with, and by the ways I have learned to look at the world as a result of my experiences with others.

While you might think of me as the lone author of this book, I am not alone. I am writing as the relational intersection of all these influences. And you, as the reader, bring your own intersections with you in how you read it, what you perceive, and what you take from it. So, in encountering this book, you aren't encountering *me*, you are encountering *we*, which includes you as well.

It was a passage about relation that started penetrating the darkness on my flight to Germany. My fundamental mistake had been that, despite all my convictions to the contrary, I had still bought into ideas that could too easily be misunderstood in individualistic, nonrelational ways. Alone, this is not surprising, as the conceptual air we all breathe is still overwhelmingly individualistic in its assumptions, despite the fact that science has completely debunked individualistic theories in favor of relational ones. On that flight, I suddenly saw something with great clarity, something I believe the world will soon come to understand as well: *Management of the individual is dead, or soon will be; management of relation is the new leadership paradigm.*

In 2021, I founded a new firm, Withiii Leadership, to keep exploring and pushing down this new path of understanding. The ideas in *You and We* capture what we at Withiii do to help organizations and their people. They are powerful ideas and approaches for bringing people together, whether in companies, neighborhoods, or on the world stage, as they don't presume the very divides that people are trying to overcome. Rather, they are built on and powered by *relation*.

I have written *You and We* in the same style I used when writing *Leadership and Self-Deception* and *The Anatomy of Peace*—as a story. If you are familiar with those earlier books, you will no doubt recognize my voice. While I draw much inspiration from stories and people I have encountered throughout my life, the characters in *You and We* are fictional. Having said that, I find myself in every single one of them. My hope is that you will discover parts of yourself in these characters as well—in Zane, Dot, Cree, Eliza, Pam, Ricardo, and the rest. As you do, their wrestling and discoveries will become yours as well, and you will become the most important character in the story.

You and We is a culmination of all I have learned over my years researching, training, advising, mentoring, and working with leaders to transform their organizational ecosystems. In a way, it is a powerful 2.0 to my earlier works—a work that attempts to correct misconceptions and move understanding and application forward in even more dynamic directions. It details not only the best way I have learned to lead and run organizations, but also the best method for stitching the human family together in the face of our many threats.

This book is a journey into the art and science of relation, applied to work, to life, and to leadership. It's about *you* and about *we*, and about how *together* wins. However, as you will discover, *together* doesn't mean what you think it does. And the way we get there may be a path you've never before considered.

PART I

A New Paradigm

1

The Chosen

Zane Savage silently pumped his fist as he looked out over the standing-room-only crowd in Bellweather Labs' new auditorium. All the battles he had waged to make this gathering and setting a reality were now being vindicated. He believed the company was finally turning a corner and that doubts people had about the organization's direction, and about him as its leader, would soon disappear.

Zane was the 44-year-old son of Bellweather's founder, Frank Savage. He had been leading the company for three years, with mixed results. On the one hand, company performance had remained solid. But there also was a sense of unease in the organization—a feeling that they had somehow lost their way.

Under Zane's leadership, Bellweather had moved its headquarters to Alexandria, Virginia, across the Potomac River from Washington, DC. In his view, proximity to DC was essential for the company's growth and strategy over the coming decades, as Bellweather's work in quantum computing had enormous national and international security implications.

The move wasn't popular with employees, however. It was announced in the immediate aftermath of the sudden retirement of the company's beloved longtime CEO, Dorothy "Dot" Kessler. And, for many of them, it meant leaving the corporate campus home they had built in the hills of Pittsburgh, Pennsylvania. Families would be uprooted, spouses forced to make career adjustments, and children would face the loss of their entire friend groups.

Despite a turbulent political climate that had everyone on edge, Zane kept assuring people that everything would work out. "These are the right moves. You'll see."

However, Zane's outward confidence hid two personal realities. First, inwardly, he was hurt by what he perceived as others' lack of confidence in him, both as the chief architect of the new corporate strategy and now as the head of the company. Secondly, he bristled over the affection for Dot Kessler that still coursed through the veins of the workforce.

If Dot were a blood type, it was like the entire company was D positive. This allegiance, more than any of the myriad corporate challenges they had faced over the three years since Dot had stepped away, kept Zane up at night. He was famous for barely sleeping and for writing scores of music for imagined Broadway musicals in the fitful early morning hours. What people didn't know was that it was the ghost of Dot's shadow that chased his sleep away and energized his music. To secure the respect he believed he deserved, Zane felt he had to be more than she was. It was that thought, and the unfairness of it, that haunted his sleep.

If any shadow deserved to tower over him and the company, Zane thought, it was his father's. Frank Savage had died only four years earlier while still serving as chairman of the board. The fact that company employees felt more allegiance to and affection for Dot Kessler than Frank Savage irked Zane. It was also evidence, he believed, that Dot had failed to give his father the public respect and deference he deserved. Her ascendancy as the face of Bellweather's brand felt like an eraser to the family's name. His bitterness over this had developed over such a long period of time that he remained almost entirely unaware that his animus about Dot's success and public reputation was what ultimately caused him to push her out the door.

What some whispered was a coup started quietly. Zane had become particularly close with two of his colleagues on the executive team. They met frequently behind closed doors to explore possibilities for the company and to discuss strategy. These efforts intensified after his father died. Out of these secret exchanges, a new vision for the company and its mission eventually burst like a flame into their minds. Convinced that the future of Bellweather could be way bigger than even Dot had been envisioning, they began to talk about how she was holding them back.

As cracks between Dot's and Zane's visions for the company began surfacing, Zane used the weight and enthusiasm of his allies to drive a wedge into the gap between them. A battle for control of the company erupted at the board level. Faced with the prospect of losing either the longtime CEO who was nearing retirement or the hard-charging son of the company's founder, the board warmed to Zane's vision. While Dot offered to stay on the board as Zane's father had, Zane wouldn't allow it.

When Dot announced her departure and retirement to an utterly stunned workforce, it was met with shock and disbelief. Bellweather Labs without her was unimaginable.

Which, to Zane, was exactly the problem.

He shrugged off the memories of those harder days. Today was the beginning of a new era. As he waited the final moments to take the stage in the auditorium bearing his father's name, the world was finally lining up the way Zane had always felt it should. He might have allowed himself to cry if doing so would have made him look strong. Instead, he slammed the door on his emotions the way his ex-military father had taught him and strode onto the stage.

The room erupted in applause.

That reception, combined with the early spring light that illuminated the three-story windows on the south side of the auditorium, seemed, to Zane, to capture the moment perfectly. The future had never been brighter for Bellweather. The company his father founded was about to become a global phenomenon.

"Thank you! Thank you, everyone!" he boomed. He was smiling so broadly that his teeth virtually eclipsed the rest of his face. "Can you believe it? We're here! Bellweather has landed!" He paused for effect. "And soon, the whole world will know of our arrival!"

As the audience cheered, Zane paused for a moment to gather himself. He was a child of the theater and a student of contemporary communication masters. He carefully choreographed every word and move for maximum impact and dug deep for that now.

"My father started Bellweather in the shed in our backyard," he began. "It was just him and Earl Crandin in those days. Remember Earl? Yeah, a few of you old-timers do. Genius engineer, Earl. I was just a little kid when they started. I had no idea what they were doing back there. My friends' dads went to work every day. Mine just went out to our shed. For years, I didn't even think my dad had a job!"

Everyone laughed good-naturedly at that, as Frank Savage was notorious for working like a madman. New employees at Bellweather still heard the stories.

Zane looked up and pointed at the dome over the auditorium. "My father had a vision that has hovered over, protected, and inspired this company from its earliest days. His legacy is like the roof over our heads. And this magnificent new campus is our shed."

Zane paused again and changed tone, exchanging his high-pitched, enthusiastic voice and determined smile for the low and serious tone of a trusted professor. "Now, I know this move has been hard," he said, following the script he had practiced many times over the prior days. "I'm convinced we'll all end up seeing it as one of the smartest things we've ever done as a company, but still, I know it's been hard. And I know that the payoffs aren't yet obvious to many of you. But they're going to come, I assure you. I say that not primarily because of the shifts in our strategy or the bold move we've made to get closer to our core customers. I say it

THE CHOSEN

because of *you*—because of the way you've all pulled together even when you weren't sure you wanted to.

"So, this isn't Frank Savage's day," he declared, picking up his volume again. "And it's certainly not my day. Today, I want to salute all of *you*—for believing enough to still be here with us. It's because of *you* that the world will soon know all about Bellweather Labs!"

As the crowd cheered, the massive screen behind Zane came to life with images of Bellweather employees over the years. He moved to the left of the stage as the images rotated on the screen. People in the hall began cheering as the faces of colleagues they knew appeared. Zane nodded in satisfaction. This was playing out exactly as he had hoped.

After the images had rolled for a few minutes, Mikél Dunning, Bellweather's Chief People Officer, walked onto the stage. The cheers for her even exceeded the levels Zane had received. *The presentation had its effect*, Zane thought.

"Hello, everyone!" Mikél called out. "Welcome to the DMV!* Now's the time you've been waiting for!" she bellowed. "You've supported the company. Now it's time that the company got better at supporting you!"

At this, the Frank Savage Dome, as it had been named, was almost sent into orbit by the sheer volume of the cheering. Zane tensed up. He bristled at the implication that the company hadn't been supportive of its employees. Furthermore, he was uncomfortable with what was about to happen next, as it violated his inclination to carefully manage and control outcomes.

Four people of the employees' choosing would now be enrolled in a unique program to advance their leadership skills, joining leaders from other organizations in the DMV area to make an intimate cohort of 12 leaders. The best practices shared across these organizations and the relationships built during the program were meant to benefit each of them and, as a result, Bellweather as a whole.

---

* The DMV is what DC-area folks call the greater DC area, consisting of DC, Maryland, and Northern Virginia.

Mikél had argued that no parameters should be placed on employee voting, enabling them to vote for anyone they wanted, and for any reason. For Zane, that lack of direction and intentionality amounted to a huge missed opportunity. Mikél pushed back that employees had only been on the receiving end of the company's directives over the last three years. Allowing them to decide how they wanted to load the leadership program was a meaningful way to give them a voice. Zane disagreed, but Mikél, to his astonishment, won the argument with the executive team.

"You remember how you nominated colleagues from around the company for advanced leadership training?" Mikél called out to the crowd. Everyone nodded enthusiastically.

"We're going to announce those winners right now."

On cue, a Sikorsky VH-3D Sea King helicopter, similar to Marine One that transports the president of the United States, began descending on the lawn beyond the bank of windows. Zane had instructed his team well. Everything was choreographed for effect.

"I have your votes right here!" Mikél shouted when an envelope was passed to her. "We used outside accountants—beauty pageant style—to gather your inputs. No one in the company, including me, has seen the results. We're all going to hear them together.

"If your name is called," she continued, "please gather to my left in front of the stage. You see that bird out there?" she asked, pointing at the Sikorsky. "The four nominees will be boarding it, as their training will begin immediately."

This was met with complete surprise. Eyes and mouths hung wide open all around the hall.

"With that, here are the names!"

Mikél opened the envelope. "Okay, name number one: our COO, Judy Li!"

Good choice, Zane thought to himself. *A pretty able leader but with room to grow.*

"Number two: Rita Johnson."

THE CHOSEN

Zane's heart fell. Rita managed their largest factory. And she was a problem. Maybe his number one nemesis, in fact. *She's going to paint an ugly picture of us*, he groused to himself. *And unfairly. On the other hand,* he reasoned, *maybe the program can talk some sense into her.*

"Number three: Cree Evans, Chief of Engineering!"

Zane looked out at the crowd to locate Cree. This one was interesting. On the one hand, he was a first-rate engineer. But he'd only been in this position for six months, and it was clear that his engineering and leadership abilities were inversely related. He was a bit of an odd duck, and people were complaining. Zane was close to replacing him.

"And finally, number four!"

Mikél looked down at the list and paused, as if working to make sure she got the name right. She finally raised her head and focused her eyes straight ahead into the crowd.

"Zane Savage!"

2

Questions

Zane peered numbly out the window toward the west as the Sikorsky began its climb out of Alexandria. Bellweather's campus disappeared behind them as they took a north to northwesterly path along the Potomac River. In another two minutes, the views out the windows to the east would rival any in the United States—the Lincoln Memorial, Washington Monument, and Capitol Building lining up in a grand procession from one end of the National Mall to the other. Although Zane never tired of this view, it was the furthest thing from his mind at the moment.

Zane had been the last to board. Two single chairs at the front left of the cabin, which faced each other as seats in trains sometimes do, had been unoccupied. He had seated himself in the one facing forward. His three colleagues had distributed themselves across the two couches against the opposite wall. Perhaps they avoided sitting in either of the chairs because they didn't want to risk sitting eye-to-eye with their CEO. Or maybe they liked the space and uniqueness of being able to hurtle through the air on sofas. Either way, Zane was happy for 15 minutes of relative privacy.

He looked down at the envelope in his hands. PLEASE OPEN ON THE FLIGHT, it read. He turned it over and over. *What a waste of my time*, he thought to himself.

"You look happy to be here, Zane."

Judy Li, Bellweather COO, was sitting on the couch directly opposite him, taunting him with a smile.

Zane conjured a smile in return. "Thrilled. You, too, I suppose, Judy?"

"I'm not too surprised," she answered. "Cracking heads doesn't make you a lot of friends. Especially if you're a woman."

"I don't know," Zane responded. "I rather think this was a popularity contest. But listen, there will likely be some important people in the other groups. We need to be at the top of our game."

Judy nodded.

"Shall we?" Zane asked, lifting his envelope.

They opened their envelopes, each of which contained a card with the following:

BEFORE ARRIVING, PLEASE—

A. Think of two relationships in your life: (1) one of your best; and (2) one of your worst.
B. For each relationship, list three words that describe you in that relationship.

Hmm, I'm not exactly sure where Mikél is going with this, Zane thought. Then he remembered that she had purposely remained silent about their leadership training partner. *"Can't give anyone any advantages,"* she had said, coyly. *"But I think it will be the most unique and powerful leadership course anyone in the company has ever experienced."*

Zane was skeptical of that. Bellweather was renowned for a proven leadership training approach that his father started, and that Dot had continued after him—one-on-one training and mentoring for every leader in the company, mid-level managers and up. Although they hadn't quite kept up with the program over these three years of upheaval, the foundational contours were still firmly in place. He doubted anything could top what they were already doing. Scrupulous person that he was, however, he grabbed a pen to complete his prework.

The name that immediately came to mind for his best relationship was Jacob Halliday—or "Hal," as Zane called him. Hal was Bellweather's Chief Product Officer. Zane's senior by five years, Hal had mentored him from Zane's earliest days in the company. Zane's father had personally asked Hal to take Zane under his wing. And he had. They had worked together now for almost 20 years, and Hal never once made Zane feel beneath him, even in the early days when Zane was by any measure a human fixer-upper project. By the same token, despite being the founder's son, Zane had never lorded over Hal, even as he ascended the company ladder. They were friends. Zane would do anything for him.

Okay, what words would describe me in this relationship? Zane thought about it for a minute and decided on the following: *Trusting. Grateful. Indebted.*

Now for his worst relationship. This one was even more obvious. Zane's marriage, such as it was, had been hanging by a thread for years. His wife, Laney, had recently filed for divorce and had quietly moved into her own place near Georgetown University, while Zane stayed in their historic Alexandria row house. No one else knew yet, not even their two kids, who were away at school. Zane wasn't sure if anyone would ask for the piece of paper he was writing his words on, so he used a fictitious name—a man's name at that—just in case the card fell into the wrong hands. Instead of Laney, he wrote "John." The descriptive words came easily: *Angry. Humiliated. Rejected.*

Zane looked out the window, trying to push Laney from his mind. He knew where they were going. He just hadn't thought he'd be part of the trip. At that moment, they were crossing into Maryland near Cabin John. They soon would be flying over the venerable Congressional Country Club. Zane was a hack golfer, but he had been invited to play Congressional twice since relocating to DC. Last time out, his left-handed slice had actually struck a car on Persimmon Tree Road, which, unfortunately for that car and driver, paralleled the course precisely where Zane was wildly swinging.

A few minutes beyond Congressional, amid the rolling hills of Potomac, Maryland, they would arrive at their destination: a 300-acre, privately owned contemporary art museum and nature refuge called Glenstone, the brainchild of billionaire philanthropists Mitchell and Emily Rales.

Minutes later, the Sikorsky passed over the top of Glenstone's main museum complex from the south. Zane could see a fleet of black SUVs in the preserve's parking lot a little farther to the north. *It looks like the others have arrived already,* he thought to himself. *Not in such grand fashion, though!*

The native grasses that crowned the grounds and hills below and around them began bending and dancing wildly as they started to descend. Suddenly realizing he hadn't acknowledged anyone on the helicopter except Judy, Zane snapped out of his internal stupor. He spun his seat around to look at Cree and Rita, who were on the couch toward the back. "Okay, people!" he said, smiling broadly. "You excited?"

"About as excited as I suspect you are, Boss," Rita answered without returning the smile.

Zane tried to hide his dislike, both of Rita and the situation. "You kidding? This is the kind of opportunity you get only once or twice in a career. World-class thought leadership and training, stunning venue, and the opportunity to form relationships with some of the most highly placed power brokers in the country."

"Who are you talking about?" Cree asked.

This provided an opening for Zane to share something he found intriguing about the event. "We'll be joining two other groups here. Four people from Capitol Hill—two each from the House and the Senate, I believe, and then another four leaders from some other organization around the greater DC area."

"The same way we were voted here?" Rita asked. "The senators were voted here? And the congresspeople? By whom?"

Zane shook his head. "I'm not sure, exactly. I've been asking myself the same question. Some group powerful enough—maybe with money enough—to get people's attention, that's what I'm thinking."

"Sounds like agents of the Deep State," Cree interjected.

Zane chuckled. "I hear that term a lot, Cree, but I've never met anyone who can point me to who they actually are."

"Exactly," Cree responded.

Zane laughed again. "Well, then I guess you can do some investigative work over the next couple of days, Cree. But don't forget to make a good impression, even while you're snooping. It will help the company if these people think well of us."

"But why are *we* here?" Judy followed up. "Almost every major company in the country has at least some presence in the area. Why is Bellweather involved? Are we the ones putting it on?"

Never thinking he would have anything to do with the event, Zane hadn't given it much thought. Mikél had driven everything. *"It'll be a good perk for the employees,"* she had assured him. *"And those who end up going will have the opportunity to improve their leadership in ways that may really help us."* No, Bellweather wasn't behind this. But Zane never thought to ask Judy's question: Why *was* Bellweather selected to be here? He didn't actually know.

"No, it's not us," Zane answered. "We're participants here just like everyone else." Still puzzling over the question, he added, "Let's make the best of it, shall we? Maybe it will be great."

By now they had touched down, and the door opened, revealing the stairs. "Welcome to Glenstone, everyone!" came a voice from outside. "Please make your way to the entrance hall in the building straight ahead of you."

Zane stepped to the helicopter's open door and froze.

Below him, at the base of the stairs, stood Dot Kessler.

3

Surprises

Hello, Zane."

Zane hadn't seen Dot since the day they signed papers finalizing her departure. They hadn't interacted in any way since. He was thunderstruck, and momentarily speechless.

Regaining his form, he bounded down the stairs with his signature electric smile. "Dot! Wow! What an incredible surprise. How have you been?" The pitch of his voice rose unnaturally, as if squeezing the air through smaller pipes.

"I've been well, Zane," she answered warmly, her brows creasing together the way they always did in conversation. "It's good to see you. How about you? How have you been? How are Laney and the kids? And how's the Bellweather team?"

"Ahh, we're all good," Zane lied. "It's a crazy time with the move and all, but everything's great."

"That's terrific to hear, Zane. I can't wait to learn more over the next couple of days." She patted him on the back.

"Welcome, everyone!" she said, as the rest were now descending the steps.

Judy and Rita, who had worked with Dot for years, called out her name almost in unison. "Dot!" They rushed to her and embraced.

"We're here with *you*?" Judy asked. "How awesome is that!"

"I'm the lucky one, Judy. It's wonderful to see you—Rita, you too." She then extended her hand in welcome to Cree. "I don't think we've met. Dot Kessler. It's really good to have you here."

"Cree Evans. I've heard a lot about you, ma'am. Even the engineers tell the stories. You're kind of a mythical figure around the company—like Zeus or something."

"Oh, goodness." Dot laughed. "I'm not sure it ended well for Zeus, did it? I'm not certain he's still around." She chuckled again and glanced with a smile at Zane. "Maybe I *am* a bit like Zeus, then." She looked back at Cree. "But please, call me Dot."

Zane fidgeted. But he knew he wasn't the only one feeling anxious. Dot, effortlessly smooth and carefree in normal circumstances, had a tell when she was feeling nervous. Her right hand came to her face, sometimes just brushing her nose or wiping at the side of her mouth. And she just did that. He stepped in to take control.

"The others are here?" he asked.

"Yes, everyone arrived over the last 30 minutes or so. Although no one quite like you," she added. She smiled warmly again. And no hand to her face.

"Yes, well, it seemed like a good idea," Zane said.

"Oh, for sure! You're in DC, why not travel like the president? When in Rome, you know! I try to hop a ride on Marine One whenever I can."

Zane looked at her. He wasn't sure she was joking.

Dot fell into conversation with the others as they walked toward the entrance. The straight-lined modern architecture and gray-colored stone of the complex rose and fell in blocks against the sky. It was a striking sight against the waving grasses, plants, and trees of the natural surroundings. But Zane took almost no notice of any of it. He was focused on one thing and one thing alone: *What is Dot Kessler doing here? Is this her program? Is Mikél in cahoots with her? And have I been set up?*

In the entrance hall, Dot asked them to stop and take note of the words etched prominently on the wall in front of them:

Substance so stirred at its depth
To result in a change in essence
Opening a path for transformation
From solitariness
To synthesis[5]

"What do you get from those words?" Dot asked them.

After a moment's silence, Judy spoke up. "Not much, actually. It's talking about change, I suppose, but I'm not sure what to make of the rest of it. It reads like science that's trying to make itself into poetry. Not sure it works."

The others nodded.

"Over the next few minutes before we begin," Dot said, "I invite you to ponder how this verse might apply to you, even if it strikes you as strange. And how, collectively, it might also apply to Bellweather."

Zane glanced at the words again before turning for the stairs. Dot sidled up next to him. "I'm not much into poetry, Dot," he said as they walked. "And I'm not sure what those words have to do with Bellweather, either, to be honest."

She nodded. "Anyone as serious about music as you are, Zane, has poetry in their soul. I'll be interested in what you have to say about those words by tomorrow."

"Yeah, maybe," he demurred.

They reached the bottom of the stairs.

"Maybe think about it this way," she said. "How does the verse illuminate how your current strategies at Bellweather are going to fail?"

Zane stopped in his tracks. "That's what you think, Dot? That we're going to fail?" He chuckled. "I'd suggest you're way too far away at this point to know."

"*Too far away.*" Dot nodded with a calm but serious expression. "That's exactly why you are currently set up to fail, Zane. And failure, given what Bellweather potentially has to offer, is something that vital sectors of the economy, not to mention this nation and other nations, can't afford to have happen."

Zane was incredulous. "You couldn't be more wrong. Everything we're doing—moving here to DC included—is about getting closer to who we need to be close to."

"Proximity is not closeness, Zane. After working together for years, that should be clear to both of us, don't you think?" She smiled in a way that unnerved him. "But don't worry. There's nothing we're going to talk about that doesn't apply as much to me as to you. And, though you may not believe it now, I'm rooting for you. Counting on you, actually."

Somehow, Zane didn't take any comfort in that.

Resuming walking, they turned a corner to a long hallway. The left wall was entirely glass all the way down, looking out onto a huge internal courtyard of ponds and tall grasses. They came to the end of the hall and bent to the right around a short corner. A din of conversations pulled them into a room to the left.

The room was like none Zane had ever seen before. There was no wall to the outside, just an empty threshold, the other side of which was the breezy landscape of the museum's hundreds of acres. It was a spectacular setting. *But there's no breeze,* Zane realized. He walked over to the threshold, and then he saw it was another huge pane of glass extending the entire length of the room. It had been engineered and placed in such a way as to create an illusion of intimate connection to the outside. Zane wasn't easily impressed, but the effect was almost bewitching. The space was both a room and not a room, at the same time.

"Zane Savage." Zane turned to the voice.

It was Senator Arlo Summers, Republican of Maryland, and ranking member of the Senate's Armed Services Committee.

"Hello, Senator," Zane said, beaming. "What a pleasure!"

"If I could have everyone's attention for a moment," Dot called out. "Thank you so much for coming! We're going to begin in five minutes. Until then, I would invite you to please circulate the room and learn as many of each other's names as you can. Five more minutes of conversation, okay? Then we'll get started."

People complied good-naturedly. The conversations were brief but cordial, and most everyone was able to at least exchange greetings. For his part, Zane concentrated on those who seemed most important to him—Senators Summers and Wilkes, Congressman Alton, and Congresswoman Schuler. He hadn't had time to meet the rest and didn't know who they were.

"Please be seated, everyone," Dot called out again. "Anywhere you'd like is fine."

Within a minute or so, all were seated and ready. A curious silence settled in the room.

"Welcome to Glenstone," Dot said warmly. "What an amazing group you are!" She glanced at Zane when she said this, unnerving him once again. "In this group, we have four leaders from my former company, Bellweather Labs, including my successor as CEO, Zane Savage, four members of Congress, and four executives from PERC—Public Electric Reliability Corporation—who are responsible for ensuring the reliability of the nation's power grid."

Zane looked around the room to locate the PERC executives. He wanted to make sure he got to know them. They needed what Bellweather had to offer.

"You are all doing really important work," Dot continued, "work that affects not only you and the lives of your employees, but that potentially affects people across the country in very profound ways.

"Which brings us to why we are here. The short answer is that we are part of an experiment, commissioned by the White House, to see how we can build bridges within and across different sectors of the economy and community. There is concern, shared by many across the political and economic spectrums, that the fabric of society is breaking down. The economic data shows that figuring out how to bring people together is as critical for national strength and security as are technological innovation on the one hand and strong defense capabilities on the other. That's why forces from outside the country are investing so heavily in disinformation and other tactics designed to drive wedges between people and groups to splinter and weaken our society. There is a concerted effort to cause our sociopolitical system to implode, and the situation is far more serious than most people know. What we're doing here is part of a multi-pronged initiative to increase dialogue and connections across societal divides, and to strengthen key sectors and organizations within the economy in an effort to equip them—inoculate them, even—against forces that might otherwise divide them and undermine their commercial and social efforts."

"So, this is kind of a vaccine, then," Cree said. "You're giving us some kind of shot." Zane rolled his eyes. *Don't go crazy on me here, Cree,* he pleaded to himself.

Dot broke out into a big grin. "No, Cree. No vaccines here. Of any variety. Just a lot of honest thinking, open dialogue, and practical learning. The stakes are high. We have a lot to do."

"What's the objective for these two days?" Judy asked.

"By the end of tomorrow," Dot replied, "we hope you will not only understand why pulling together across divides is crucial for your economic survival, but that you also will have begun a transformation into leaders who can overcome the fissures that are weakening your organizations and our nation."

"Why *us* in particular?" Judy asked, repeating the question she had earlier asked Zane. "Out of all the people in the DMV, why us 12 instead of others?"

"This is the first of what we hope will be many cohort groups," Dot answered, "so you aren't alone, Judy. But we've started with you for two reasons. First, your work has been classified as essential for national

SURPRISES
23

security reasons. The second reason is because your organizations are fraying, and that collective weakness is a major threat."

"Excuse me?" Zane spoke up, his face beginning to flush. "I agree that Congress is a mess—no offense to our esteemed legislators here," he said, glancing around the room. "Capitol Hill is broken; we all know it. And for the good of the country, we all hope you can get your acts together. Again, no offense." He looked back toward Dot. "I might say the same thing about the White House, Dot. But Bellweather is in great shape. I don't know where you're getting your information from, but we're not fraying at all, and I resent the accusation that we are."

Zane shrunk back into his seat upon hearing the tone of his voice. He had a prodigious temper. In most cases, he found it helped in getting people to do as he wished, and he actually considered it an asset. In this moment, however, although frustrated by what Dot had implied, he chided himself for failing to keep his cool.

Rita snickered. "I'm sorry, Zane, but if you don't think we're divided, you're not paying attention."

Zane was now hyperconscious of his surroundings. He wanted to quell this and tried to put on a calm demeanor. "I actually don't see us that way, Rita. But that's probably a longer conversation. Let's talk about it later today—on a break or something. I want to understand your view."

"Do you?"

"Yes, of course."

"Well, I'll just say this much now, then: I used to feel valued at the company—the whole manufacturing division did, in fact. But not anymore. We're treated more like subcontractors than valued team members now. When Dot was here," she said, gesturing toward her, "she visited and consulted with us all the time. You, on the other hand, haven't visited any of our manufacturing facilities since the day you took over Dot's job. Not one time. That doesn't sound like division to you?"

Zane's neurons were now fully firing, but in two entirely different directions. On the one hand, he couldn't allow Rita's outrageous insubordination to go unchallenged. On the other hand, he had to maintain his composure to preserve his own and his company's reputation in the minds of everyone else in the room. But since Rita had made her statements in front of the group, he felt he had to respond in front of the group as well.

He put on his professor voice. "Point taken about visiting the factories, Rita. I have spent most of the last three years pivoting Bellweather into a new direction in quantum computing—a direction that will require a very different manufacturing base than we currently have. I admit that I've probably seemed absent to you and your colleagues in the factories. That's actually been by design as I haven't wanted to distract any attention away from our legacy business. It sounds like you've interpreted my absence in the factories as me not caring, when, in fact, it actually means that I trust you and what you are doing."

Rita didn't respond immediately, and Zane counted that as a win. He meant what he said about not wanting to distract the team from the legacy business. But he didn't trust Rita and was regretting that he hadn't already fired her.

"I'm not sure I totally agree with you, Zane," Judy spoke up.

Not now, Judy! he thought. *Let it go!*

"I know that we haven't wanted to disrupt the current operations," she continued, "and I think that's been the right strategy. But I think we could find ways to be more transparent about our plans and to help those who aren't yet involved in our 2.0-level efforts to still feel highly valued."

"Zane, Rita, Judy," Dot said, "thank you for sharing these initial thoughts. I really appreciate the transparency. If it's okay with you, I'd like to park this discussion for now and perhaps come back to it when we have more insights to leverage. Would that be all right with you?"

"Absolutely," Zane said, grateful to have the spotlight removed. "Let's move on." The others agreed.

"Okay, then. Everyone, if you would, please take out the cards where you listed words describing how you are in two different relationships in your life."

Zane pulled his out of his pocket.

WITH HAL	WITH JOHN
Trusting	Angry
Grateful	Humiliated
Indebted	Rejected

"My question for each of you is this: Are the words you chose to describe Relationship 1 the same words you chose for Relationship 2?"

Everyone in the room shook their heads.

"So, your lists are completely different?"

People nodded.

"Isn't that to be expected?" Zane asked. "Is the difference supposed to mean something?"

"As we'll discover together, Zane," Dot answered, "it means that the world isn't at all what we think it is."

4

The Only Thing We See

I want to introduce you to someone," Dot said, motioning to the back of the room. "I'd like you to meet my good friend and colleague Ricardo Bloom. Ricardo is a physicist at MIT. And," she added, "no doubt the smartest person in the room."

"No, no, no, I reject that out of hand!" Ricardo protested. "Honestly, I'm feeling intimidated just being here with all of you."

"As I said," Dot interjected, "the most naturally gifted politician in the room!"

Everyone laughed at that.

Everyone except Zane. He hadn't recognized the now bearded and spectacled Ricardo Bloom. Ricardo had been one of Zane's early targets for Bellweather's board of scientific advisors. Two years earlier, after a few conversations, he had even traveled to Cambridge, Massachusetts, to woo and offer him the post. Although their meeting had been genial, Ricardo declined every offer. When Zane asked what it would take to attract him to Bellweather, Ricardo had simply said, "Something you aren't prepared to give."

28   YOU AND WE

"Try me," Zane had responded, expecting a request for equity.

"I already did," was Ricardo's cryptic response.

There was no budging him. Nothing Zane said seemed to matter. For reasons opaque to him, Ricardo wasn't interested in Bellweather.

So, I'm here with someone I ousted and another who ghosted me. Wonderful! Zane's thoughts turned again to Mikél who, he guessed, must also have known about Ricardo's involvement.

"Well, then," Ricardo began. "Let's continue with the discussion Dot just introduced." He raised his own card, which he himself had filled out. "If the words that describe you in each of your relationships are different, it raises an interesting question. Namely: *Which person are you?* Are you the person you described in your good relationship or the person you described in your difficult one?"

Texas congresswoman Eliza Schuler, the Republican Majority Whip in the House, whose name was just one letter shy of matching the name of Alexander Hamilton's famous spouse, spoke up. "I suppose I'm both," she said.

"Great, thank you," Ricardo said. "And since we haven't met before, can I ask if it would be okay if I call you Eliza?"

"Been called a lot worse!" she replied. "No, but seriously, I'd prefer it. We don't do formal in Texas."

"How about for all you non-Texans?" Ricardo asked the rest of the group. "Would it be okay if we all call each other by our first names? It just feels more real that way."

Everyone nodded.

"Okay, excellent. So, then, Eliza, you said you're *both* of those people."

"That's right."

"So, what does that mean?"

"Well, in Texas, it means you shouldn't mess with me."

Everyone laughed again, breaking the ice still more.

The truth was, Eliza Schuler had a reputation as a sweet-talking pit bull, so the idea of two entirely different descriptive lists for her made perfect sense. One of the Republican Party's most recognizable national

THE ONLY THING WE SEE 29

faces and voices, who had flirted with running for president during the last cycle, she was a frequent guest on national news shows, where she charmed viewers and hosts alike. On the flip side, she was House Whip because of her willingness and ability to apply pressure wherever and whenever it was needed. She was one of the most powerful people on Capitol Hill.

"I'm going to introduce you to what is perhaps the central development in science over the last century—a relational understanding of reality," Ricardo said. "It has profound implications for human beings, both individually and collectively. But don't worry, I'm not going to blow you out with the science. If you want a more strictly scientific explanation of what I'm going to give you, I'll point you to where you can get it.[6] But the approach I will take with you today is to introduce that science through four analogies. Each analogy will yield one law of relation, and I think the four of them together will help us cut through much of the mistaken conceptual air that we breathe that is holding us back in the way we engage the world around us. When we understand all four laws of relation, we'll be ready to apply a relational understanding to people and organizations and will dive into real-life applications, which is what we'll spend most our time doing together.

"For our first analogy, I need a volunteer."

Eliza raised her hand.

"Very good, Eliza. Could you join me up here for a second?"

"You promised—no science, right?" she probed with a smile.

"No worries," Ricardo answered with a chuckle. "I just want to play a little tic-tac-toe with you."

"Let's go, cowboy." She joined him at the front of the room.

Ricardo drew the familiar grid on a flip chart. "Okay, then I'll go first," he said.

"Surprise, surprise," she replied.

Ricardo placed an X in the upper left corner. Eliza thought about it and drew an O in the middle. Ricardo then placed an X in the bottom right corner, to which Eliza responded by drawing an O in the bottom left. "Ahh, thank you," Ricardo said. He placed an X in the upper right,

YOU AND WE

trapping her. He would either get three across the top or three down the right side. Eliza could block only one direction.

"Okay, again!" she said. "That was a warm-up."

"Fair enough." Ricardo drew a second grid. He again started with an X in the upper left corner. This time Eliza placed an O in the side space directly beneath Ricardo's X. He then placed a second X in the upper right corner. Eliza blocked him by drawing an O in the center top between his two X's. Then Ricardo placed his third X in the bottom right corner.

"Ah, shit," Eliza said, laughing. She was trapped again. Ricardo could beat her either diagonally or down the right side. "If the speaker saw this, I'd be out of a job!"

Ricardo busted out laughing. "I very much doubt *that*!" he said. "It's just a meaningless game, after all. However, win or lose, it does illustrate something of fundamental importance—of scientific importance, actually. Think about it this way: In our first game, your first move was in the middle. Why did you go there?"

"Well, I thought it was a good move after you first went corner."

"Smart," Ricardo said. "In fact, middle is the only safe countermove to a corner-first start. So, you put your O in the center because I put my X in the corner."

"Exactly."

"The same was true for my next move," Ricardo continued. "I chose bottom-right corner because I thought it was my best remaining move after you went middle."

"Okay," Eliza said. "So?"

"Every move in the game is relational," Ricardo replied. "No move stands on its own. You placed your O's where you did in response to where I placed my X's, and I placed my X's in response to your O's. Even the first moves I made were in anticipation of what I thought you might do in response. So, every move in the game is in response to other moves. You are in *my* moves, and I am in *yours*. Everything that is happening in the game is relational. Does that make sense?"

"Yeah, I get it."

THE ONLY THING WE SEE

"Then you are ready for the First Law of Relation: *Everything you see is relation.*"

"Could you explain what you mean by *relation*?" Zane asked.

"Hey, Zane. Good to see you again," Ricardo replied.

That's the second time I've been lied to today with the exact same words, Zane thought to himself.

"And great question. The meaning of *relation* is what we're just beginning to explore. For now, I'll say this much: Everything being in relation means that nothing stands on its own. Everything depends on something else. We think we're seeing *things*, when what we're actually seeing are intersecting activities or relations."

Eliza squinted. "I'm not sure I understand what that means."

"Go ahead and sit down, and we'll talk about it."

Eliza took her seat.

"Okay, everyone, let's think about this. Look around the room for a moment. You think you are seeing things and people—that window, for example, the screen up here, the chairs we're sitting on, and, most significantly, each other. But, in fact, all you are really seeing is *relation*. And I want to demonstrate that by having all of us look at Zane for a moment."

"Great!" Zane said in mock protest.

Ricardo laughed. "Just for a moment! When you're looking at Zane, what are you seeing?" Ricardo asked.

"Is it appropriate to say that out loud?" Eliza joked.

Everyone cracked up. "Please, keep it to yourself," Zane played along.

"Do you want us to *describe* Zane?" Rita asked.

"No, I just want you to tell me what you are seeing when looking at him."

"I don't know what you mean by that," Rita said. "I'm seeing *Zane*!"

"On the contrary," Ricardo said. "You *think* you are, but you're actually not."

"Is this some kind of weird puzzle or something?" Cree asked.

Ricardo smiled. "Not at all, Cree. When I look at a person—at Zane in this case—I think I am seeing Zane. But what I am missing is the fact that *I* am seeing Zane. And since *I* am the person who is seeing, I'm not seeing a world that is separate from me but am rather seeing my own interaction with the world. So, what I'm seeing is not Zane per se, but rather my relational intersection with him. In fact, relationality goes even further than that. It's not just that *I* am seeing Zane; it's also that I'm seeing a *Zane* who is in response to *me*.

"Of all the lessons in science over the last century, this is the most important one, and I would suggest that it's the most important leadership lesson as well: When we observe and measure the world, we're not observing and measuring a world separate from ourselves; we're observing and measuring our own interaction or relation with the world and the world's interaction with us. As the great physicist Werner Heisenberg said, 'What we observe is not Nature itself, but Nature exposed to our method of questioning.'[7] *Everything we see is relation*—that's the First Law.

Ricardo looked around at everyone. "Does that make sense?"

People nodded. "Yeah, that's actually pretty interesting," Judy said. "So, just to make sure I have this right, this means that I'm never actually experiencing *you*. Rather, I'm experiencing *myself with you*. So, in that respect, all I can ever see is relation—not things in themselves, but intersections."

"Exactly," Ricardo said. "So, the question that gets to the heart of things between people is not *Who am I?* for example, or *Who are you?* which are *thing*-based questions, but rather, *Who are you and I together? And what are we creating together?* These are relational questions.

For a moment, Zane began to consider: *Who are Judy and I together? What are we creating?* Then, in a flash, the question migrated across the landscape of his life. *Who are Ricardo and I together? Who are Dot and I together? Who are Laney and I together?*

"But relationality will take us even deeper than this," Ricardo continued. "In order to introduce the Second Law of Relation, we're going to consider a second analogy—this one contained in a painting.

"The museum just so happens to have on loan one of the epic paintings of the scientifically inclined Georges Seurat—a masterpiece called

THE ONLY THING WE SEE

A Sunday Afternoon on the Island of La Grande Jatte.[8] It's hanging in the next room, directly behind us. This painting is particularly famous because it marked a new approach called 'pointillism,' which inspired van Gogh, Picasso, and many other modern masters. The word *pointillism* references the unique way the painting was constructed by using only small dots. Seurat didn't mix colors or use brushstrokes to produce the overall colors or to construct the scene. Instead, over a two-year period, he painted it by applying hundreds of thousands of distinct marks on the canvas—dots that, together, create the world of the painting.

"We're going to take 30 minutes for this. I invite you to spend some time with Seurat's masterpiece. As you take the painting in, consider what we have been discussing about relation. Does the painting confirm that all we see is relation, or does it counter it?

"With our midmorning start today, we are getting toward lunchtime as well. So, we also have food set up for you in the hall. Enjoy the food and the painting!

"See you back here in 30 minutes."

5

The *We* Called *Me*

On break, Zane made a point of chatting up the four people from PERC, the Public Electric Reliability Corporation. They had been silent so far, so he didn't have a feel for them. They were Jorn Whistler, CEO; Tim Costello, VP of Governmental Affairs; Pam Donaldson, VP of People and Culture; and Stuart Reddy, Chief Engineer. As a group, they were a bit reserved, Zane thought, except for Pam, whose personal energy seemed a good fit for her role in their organization.

He'd heard of PERC before and knew that they were involved with the nation's energy grid, but he hadn't known any details. He learned that they were a nonprofit regulator working with energy providers across the United States and Canada. Their mission was to ensure the reliability and security of North America's power grids. They didn't operate the energy assets themselves but had administrative oversight over those who did. As a potential conduit into all the big players in the energy sector, Zane thought they could become an important partner.

Winding up his conversations, he approached Seurat's painting. It was a captivating piece, and quite large—a good ten feet wide and six or seven feet tall. Coincidentally, he actually knew of this painting, as his parents took him to a Broadway play about it when he was just a teenager. The play was called *Sunday in the Park with George*. As his first Broadway show, it left a big impression. He inched himself closer to take in the painting. Sam Alton, the Democratic congressman from California, was to Zane's left, while Bellweather's Cree Evans was to his right. They studied the painting in silence.

"Mighty impressive," Sam said after a few moments. "Incredible what he's done with all these dots. From a distance, you would never suspect it, but as you get close, the painting breaks up into a million little pieces."

"Yeah, and do you notice that the colors change as you move back?" Cree asked. "Up close, you have all these different colored dots, but as you back away, those tiny splotches of color mix together. The differences somehow play together in a way that produces colors different from any of the ingredient ones."

Zane's eyebrows rose in surprise at that—both at the observation, and at the fact that it was conspiracy-theory Cree who had made it. "Hmm, I agree, Cree. That's really interesting, actually."

"But it's also kind of an odd piece, don't you think?" It was Pam Donaldson from PERC, who was standing right behind them.

"How so?" Sam asked, glancing back to look at her.

"It looks like everyone is kind of frozen in time."

"Isn't that true of every painting to some degree?" Zane asked.

"Not like this one," Pam replied. "Look there, at the little girl above and to the right of center. She's dancing, and you can see her flow and movement. And you can see movement in the animals too. By contrast, every other figure feels like a cardboard cutout. They are stiff—standing and sitting in almost impossibly correct postures—all except for that man in entirely different kind of clothing at the bottom left who is leaning back in a much more relaxed way. And, other than that man, everyone else seems way overdressed for a day off at the river. No one else seems to be enjoying themselves at all, except for the little dancing girl. And then you have that other girl just to the left of center whose white dress is glowing in the sun. She's looking directly at us, which in a way tethers us to the scene as well, making it impossible just to keep it at a distance from us. Her eyes put *us* in the scene too."

"Wow, you're incredibly observant," Sam said. "What was the name again?"

"Pam. Pam Donaldson. I'm with PERC."

"Yes, of course. I'm Sam Alton."

Pam smiled. "I recognize you from TV."

"Yeah, what's that all about?" Cree butted in. "You politicians are getting paid to go on those shows, I suppose?"

Zane rolled his eyes. "Don't respond to that, Congressman," he said, grabbing Cree by the arm and walking him away. "I think it's time we gathered back."

Within a couple of minutes, the group had collected in the meeting room. No one was sitting down, however, as the illusion out the window was so captivating.

"Okay, everyone," Ricardo called out. "Let's gather up." They all quickly took their seats.

"Okay, then! Let's process Seurat's painting for a minute. What did you see in it? And what, if anything, does it have to do with what we've been talking about?"

"Pam, you should share what you saw in it," Sam said.

"Oh," Pam said. "Sure, okay. What struck me most was how Seurat depicted most everyone in a rigidly stiff and almost lifeless way. They're more like mannequins than people. With two exceptions, however—the dancing girl near the center of the painting and the slouching man at the bottom left of it, who actually looks comfortable and relaxed."

"Yes, Pam," Ricardo said. "That's really perceptive. Notice how your observations point us to contrasts between different elements in the painting," he continued. "It's in these contrasts between elements—that is, in the relational differences between them—that the painting communicates meaning. The contrasts raise questions: Why do almost all the people seem so stiff? What's different about those who are not? And what might those contrasts be saying? Relation between the elements is what brings the painting alive.

"And by the way," he said, "did anyone notice how devoid of facial details most of the people are—except, that is, the man Pam zeroed in on at the bottom left and the couple standing behind him? We can clearly see that the three of them are looking directly across the river, connecting us to a scene that is out of the frame. It turns out that Seurat actually painted the scene of what was happening across the river. That painting is called *Bathing at Asnières*. And when you compare the two paintings, you discover a whole new layer of meaning to both of them—meaning that is not at all obvious in isolation. Which

THE *WE* CALLED *ME*   39

means that the painting we have been considering is itself in relation to something else."

"Interesting," Cree said, almost under his breath.

"What else did you notice in the painting that pertains to what we have been discussing?" Ricardo asked.

"I'll take a crack at that, although without Pam's level of insight." It was Senator Wilkes.

"Great, Dexter, thank you."

"Well, in terms of our discussion about relation, at the granular level, I find the painting to be a bit of a contradiction. On the one hand, you have all these little dots, which feel really separate. But then, when you pull back, they all kind of converge together. So, is the painting demonstrating togetherness or independence? Is it saying that all we see is relation, or is it saying that everything is separate after all?"

Pam raised her hand. "I actually wouldn't say that the dots are separate. They are profoundly in relation, which seems to me to be the point of the entire composition."

"Great observations by both of you," Ricardo said. "Thank you. Playing off those observations, Seurat's method for this painting illuminates something really interesting about the relational nature of reality that we haven't yet mentioned. It is that everything in the world that looks like a single thing—like the painting, for example—is actually made up of other, smaller things in relation. This is true of everything in existence. Companies are made up of people in relation, for example. Sentences are made up of words in relation. Music is made up of sounds in relation. The cells of any living thing are made up of molecules in relation, which are made up of atoms in relation, which are made up of still smaller things in relation, and so on.

"These two relational truths about everything in the universe—that everything is both a whole made up of parts-in-relation while at the same time being a relational part of something even larger[9]—is what holds all the parts and layers of the universe together, including people and our organizations, just as it holds Seurat's painting together. Which brings us to the Second Law of Relation: *Everything is built by relation.*

"Seurat illustrates this point by his use of dots in relation. But what are *we* made of? What are the equivalent of Seurat's dots for *us*? A third analogy, this one from a famous experiment with light, will yield an answer."

6

Intersecting into Being

One of the most famous experiments in science," Ricardo continued, "is the so-called *double-slit* experiment designed to detect the nature of light—namely whether light is a particle or a wave.

"If you're interested in the details of the experiment, catch me on a break and I'll connect you to a good recap.[10] But for our purposes today, I will just share the results. Does anyone here know what they were?"

Cree raised his hand. "The experiment shows that light is both a particle *and* a wave."

"Yes," Ricardo said. "And depending on *what*?"

"Depending on how we interact with it," Cree replied.

"Exactly," Ricardo said. "What light is depends on how we interact with it. If we interact with it in one way, it manifests as a wave. If we interact with it in another way, it manifests as a particle. Which means that we can't say anything about light alone; we can only speak about how light is *with us*."

"That's not very satisfying," Zane objected.

"Why do you say that, Zane?"

"Because I'd like to know how light *really* is, and how the universe really is, not just how it is with *us*."

"You're in good company, Zane."

"How so?"

"Even though Einstein was the father of these discoveries, like you, he fought against the notion that there is nothing solid and unchanging beneath experience. He kept looking for the independent reality beneath everything. He kept looking, if you will, for the person you really are, independent of your relationships, and not just who you are *in* relationship. Which is to say that he kept looking for the primacy of *things* rather than *relationships*."

"And?"

"He couldn't find any such reality. In fact, no one has been able to. When you get down to the foundation of everything, at the subatomic level, things and entities disappear entirely. What all the developments in science suggest is that there is no nonrelational space. Relation is all there is. Everything in the universe manifests through intersection, interaction, and relation. Including us. That is what it means to exist. 'Nothing exists in itself,' one of my colleagues, Carlo Rovelli, has said. 'Everything exists only through dependence on something else. It is only in interactions that nature draws the world.'[11]

"So, what does that mean? I think this will start to make intuitive sense to you if you think about it in terms of the two personal relationships we each were thinking about earlier. In terms of your potentiality, you possess what physicists might call a wave of possibilities representing the countless ways you *could* show up in any given interaction or relationship. But you then show up in a particular way as you intersect with the world. At that point—at the point of intersection or relation—the possible becomes actual. Reality—who you are in the world—is birthed through relation.

"A leading humanities professor friend of mine put it this way: 'Humans always and only exist as relations. The relations don't bloom between previously pristine individuals; rather, like the particles our measurements detect, the individuals spring forth from the relations themselves.'[12] As our own little experiment around how we show up differently in our two relationships implies, we are who we show up to be in our interactions. Our interactions with others and the world are the dots that paint us.

"Which brings us to the Third Law of Relation: *How we interact is who we are.*

"But following up on what Zane was asking about earlier," Sam said, "there's a 'me' *between* interactions or relationships, isn't there?"

"That is the challenging thing for us to see," Ricardo responded. "The reason it's challenging is that relationships are to us like water is to fish. Is there any moment that I haven't had a mother, for example? Or others around me? Or memories of them? Or a world with which to interact? Since I am so continuously in relation, I experience a self that is static and continuous, but that is an illusion. The story of my 'self' is a story I tell myself that weaves together all the different ways that I intersect with and show up in the world. But that's just a story. What's real about me in the world is how I show up in these intersections with the world. I am who I am in relation, which is another way of saying that there is no me—no anything, really—independent of those relations."

"I still don't like it," Zane said.

"It's ironic, then, that you are running a company whose transformational technology is driven by this very understanding."

"How so?"

"Quantum computing is based on quantum theory, which is inherently relational, and not on classical models that standard computers use, which are thing-based.[13] It turns out that powering computers with a *relational* reality rather than a *thing*-based one unlocks massively more computational power. The question for each of us is whether we will utilize that same relational understanding to also transform our leadership and empower our organizations or, on the other hand, if we will insist on staying put in the limited world of separate, independent things."

Eliza spoke up. "Shouldn't it make us nervous that Mr. Quantum Computing here doesn't seem to understand what's powering his work?"

Although meant as a good-natured ribbing, Zane received it as an attack. "Oh, we have the science down, Eliza, you can be assured of that." Turning back to Ricardo, he added, "But with all due respect, I'm not sure your status as a scientist makes you an authority on leadership."

The words came out far sharper than he had intended, and Eliza let out a whistle. He cursed himself for making that mistake again and tried to walk his comment back. "I just mean that this is all a bit disconnected from what I deal with day to day, and I'm not sure that scientific knowledge alone makes much difference to leadership. That's all."

"Points well taken, Zane. You certainly have way more leadership experience in organizations than I do. And an understanding of science alone doesn't begin to close that gap. I couldn't agree more. However, I would submit to you that an understanding of *reality*—not science, but *reality*—is vital for good leadership. Having said that, in a couple of minutes, Dot will take the reins and help us push on what all this might mean when applied to leadership and business. She'll help us to understand what it means to manage relations rather than individuals and how powerful that approach is as a leadership paradigm.

"But before we go further in that direction, we have one more analogy and law to learn. We need to learn what kinds of relational intersections promote growth and transformation, both individually and collectively. And to consider that, I'd like to invite you to think about water."

7

Making Water

Let's imagine that all of you in this room are split into two parts," Ricardo said. "Let's suppose that those of you to my left are hydrogen atoms, while you on my right are oxygen atoms. Okay? Hydrogen atoms to my left and oxygen atoms to my right."

Everyone nodded.

"Now, you can continue forever in these two separate groups—as hydrogen and oxygen, respectively. That's just fine. But consider what happens when these two different elements combine. If they open themselves to each other and converge, the combination of hydrogen and oxygen produces something entirely new and different from either of them—something far beyond what either of them could ever imagine. The result of one version of their union is *water*: One oxygen and two hydrogen atoms combine to produce a single molecule of water, which combines with other water molecules over and over to form all the water that sustains life on this planet.

"Interestingly, there is no such thing as a water atom. Water comes into being only through the relationship of hydrogen and oxygen. And hydrogen and oxygen have to maintain their differences, even while binding with each other, in order for the miracle of water to manifest. Sameness produces nothing new. If the oxygen atom possessed the ability to change itself and decided to become a hydrogen atom like its water molecule partners, the water molecule itself would immediately disappear. Its existence depends on maintaining difference.

"This is a profoundly important point that goes way beyond water in its application. Relation itself, as we will discover, requires and depends on *difference*. Again, isolation and sameness produce nothing new. It is only through the relation of differences that anything new emerges and that higher levels of development manifest.

"Now, let's put this in more human terms. Eliza and Arlo, what is the Republican Party trying to make happen in every election cycle?"

"We're trying to win all the races, of course."

"Dexter and Sam, how about the Democrats?"

"Same thing. We think our principles and positions are the right ones, and we're trying to convince the electorate of that."

"Fair enough," Ricardo said. "Now, for a moment, let's call the Republican Party *oxygen* and the Democratic Party *hydrogen*. So, Republicans are pursuing a Congress of nothing but oxygen, and Democrats are trying to realize a hydrogen-only Congress. My question for all of us in this room is, does that sound like a good plan? Should we want that?"

"I don't want that," Jorn said. "There are one-party systems around the world, and I certainly don't want that here."

"But there are differences within parties," Cree observed, "even within single-party systems. Are you saying that no one in China is making water?"

"Well, no," Jorn responded.

"You make a good point, Cree," Ricardo said. "But is it not the same point we are making? Aren't you saying that single-party systems can make water to the degree they include differing opinions within them?"

He thought about it for a moment. "I suppose that *is* what I'm saying, yes."

MAKING WATER 47

"And, Jorn, I believe you were reacting to the idea that a Republican- or Democrat-only outcome would be bad for us precisely because it would cut down on differences—differences that are necessary in order to arrive at higher order solutions to our problems."

"Yes, exactly."

"Earlier, we considered how everything in the universe is comprised of smaller things in relation. The Fourth Law of Relation is about how that same developmental chain progresses upward. A fascinating body of work that can help us think about this is the work of the brilliant French paleontologist Pierre Teilhard de Chardin. Teilhard showed how the developmental process of everything in the universe, whether matter, life, or mind, always follows a three-part relational process. First, different things, like the oxygen and hydrogen atoms we have been discussing, *compress* against each other. Then they *converge* with each other through an internal openness to joining. You might think of this as a kind of horizontal bonding. And then, out of that convergence of difference emerges something completely new that could only come out of that relational combination—in this case, water. That is a vertical emergence of the new. This three-part process of *compression, convergence*, and *emergence* is the relational law of the universe according to Teilhard. It is the relational process that undergirds every development—not just of matter and organic life, but also the development of thought and complex human organizations.

"'We can progress only by uniting,'[14] Teilhard said. Which is why our future, he said, 'depends on the courage and resourcefulness which [people] display in overcoming the forces of isolationism, even of repulsion, which seem to drive them apart rather than draw them together.'"[15]

Ricardo looked around the room. "My guess is that each of us here, whether from Congress, Bellweather, PERC, MIT, or the White House's task force, knows something of the splintering and division that Teilhard was talking about, whether in our professional or personal lives."

Zane thought about Laney, alone in her Georgetown apartment. He had stopped even attempting to reach out to her.

YOU AND WE

"If we are going to come together more fully and productively in our lives," Ricardo continued, "it can't be by coercion, which produces only what Teilhard called a superficial pseudo-unity. 'It is inwardly that we must come together,' he said—in our depths. 'And in entire freedom.'[16]

"Which brings us to the Fourth Law of Relation: *We progress by uniting*."

Ricardo turned on the screen to display all four laws of relation.

THE LAWS OF RELATION	Analogy
1. All we see is relation.	*Tic-tac-toe*
2. Everything is built by relation.	*Seurat's painting*
3. How we interact is who we are.	*Light experiment*
4. We progress by uniting.	*Making water*

"And with that, we are ready to turn the floor over to Dot, who will begin exploring what all this means in practical terms—to us as individuals and to our organizations."

"Wait!" Dot said. "Before you yield the floor, could you share with everyone your insight about remote work that follows from what you were just talking about?"

"Oh, sure. Ever since remote and hybrid work practices emerged and became popular, organizations have been struggling to figure out how to accommodate workers' desire for work-from-home arrangements in ways that also work for companies. Teilhard's work shows that most people are asking the wrong questions around this issue. The issue isn't really between remote or in-person work. The real issue has to do with *compression*. Whether remote or in person, the vital question is: How can we organize ourselves and our work to promote the necessary *compression*, especially cross-functionally, that will generate *convergence*—the integration of separate parts into a highly functioning whole? But now I'm getting ahead of myself."

"Not at all. That's terrific, Ricardo," Dot said. "Thank you." As she walked to the front of the room, she added: "One thing that's become obvious as you've shared, Ricardo, is that even if, as was suggested, being

MAKING WATER

a great scientist doesn't necessarily equip one to be a great leader, if you're tuned into organizational issues, it certainly doesn't hurt! What a ride you've taken us on. Thank you!"

Many in the room started clapping. "Oh, he's not going anywhere!" Dot said. "You haven't heard the last from Ricardo Bloom. But that's nice of you." She added her own ovation to theirs.

"So!" Dot said, addressing the group. "With our brains now fully warmed up, let's start applying what Ricardo has shared about relation to leadership and to our work in our organizations and communities.

"Let's learn how to make water."

PART II

THINKING RELATIONALLY

8

Levels of Relation

I'd like to say a bit more about why you all were selected to be here," Dot began. "Earlier I told you that one reason was because you lead organizations that are fraying. I know that didn't land well with everyone, but the data tells the story."

"What data are you referring to?" Zane asked, his brow wrinkling. "Does the White House have secret access into our organizations or something?"

Cree nodded knowingly.

"I don't remember authorizing anything," Zane continued, oblivious to Cree's support. "And besides, as I said, although things aren't perfect at Bellweather, the company is in really good shape. Our future has never been brighter."

Dot acknowledged Zane's comment with a nod and continued. "Over the last year, our task force has been measuring the state of relations across companies and communities, heatmapping relational trends and watching for areas of worry. Part of that has been an assessment that organizations have been widely taking, including all of yours.

That instrument measures the levels of relation across different parts of your organizations and the degree to which various behavioral, attitudinal, structural, and cultural elements are inviting higher or lower levels of integration."

She turned toward Zane. "And yes, we did run that analysis at Bellweather. We worked with your Chief People Officer, Mikél Dunning. She ran the assessment across the organization. And the data shows that Bellweather is at about Congress's level. That is, your level of collaboration and integration across the company about matches what we see on Capitol Hill—slightly worse, actually."

Zane couldn't believe that Mikél had run a company assessment without his knowledge, much less one led by Dot Kessler. "No offense to our esteemed friends from the Hill," he said, "but I don't think our integration numbers could possibly be worse than theirs."

"Why would we take offense at that?" Eliza asked, grinning at Zane. "If Bellweather is as well off as you say and we are scoring at anywhere near your level, then we in Congress must be doing amazingly well! I need you out on the campaign trail for me, Zane. I'd like my constituents to have some of whatever you're having!"

Zane took a deep breath.

"Numbers are just numbers," Dot said, stepping in. "Data, as helpful as it can be, doesn't capture everything. You and your teams will have to wrestle through the numbers and decide what they mean for you— and what, if anything, you will want to do about it."

"Can we *see* the numbers, Dot?" It was Jorn Whistler, CEO of PERC. "I assume that we from PERC are here, like everyone else, because our relational scores are low—which, in our case, wouldn't surprise me, unfortunately. We've been trying to address some deep-seated cultural issues." Pam, who was PERC's VP of People and Culture, nodded in agreement.

"We'll share the numbers with you in a little while," Dot replied. "But before we do that, I need to share a set of ideas that will equip you to understand what the numbers mean.

LEVELS OF RELATION

"To begin with, I'd like you to think of an organizational chart. What would you say is the most important part of any org chart?"

"The most important part?" Judy asked.

"Yes, of any org chart," Dot replied.

"The customers?" Rita guessed.

"That's a good answer, Rita. And interesting because almost no org charts even include them. But I'm thinking of something else."

"The top leaders?"

"The people on the front lines?"

"The place where things often go wrong—middle management?"

"I see the rationale for all those answers," Dot responded. "But I would submit to you that the most important part of any org chart is actually the empty space that connects all the pieces. After all, no organization started from parts. Rather, the parts emerged out of the needs of the whole. And that whole can succeed only if those parts operate as an integrated unit. That happens, or not, in the space between us. It's in this space—in the *between*, as the philosopher Martin Buber would say[17]—that success or failure is created. Traditional, object-focused ways of leading and working focus on the parts. A relational approach to leading and working focuses on the *between*—the interaction, the space, the integration. Which begs a question: How might one chart this space? What might a *relational* org chart look like?"

Dot proceeded to share a chart with everyone in the room. It consisted of a grid, with each of the names of the people in the room listed down the left side and repeated again across the top.

"I want to introduce you to a completely different way of viewing your organizations," she said. "To do that, we're going to pretend that all of us in this room are colleagues in a business. Utilizing this chart, we're going to build a very different looking org chart for our business— a chart of the *between*.

"Now, before we fill out the chart, I want to introduce to you different ways we can be in relation with others—different relational levels, if you will. I'll describe five levels, and then we'll think about how those different relational levels will help us to construct our relational chart. As I introduce each of these levels of relation, I invite you to consider where that particular relational level might be showing up in your life or organization. Okay?"

Most in the room nodded.

"All right, then. The lowest level of relation is what we call *division*. At this level, people work at cross purposes, making things mutually harder. They actively undermine or obstruct each other. *Division*-level relationships are typically characterized by animosity, disdain, or profound distrust."

Zane's mind fixed immediately on his estranged wife, Laney. For the past decade, they had barely been on speaking terms. Car rides together were in silence. Travel together was tense, each of them trying not to light the fuse that would result in an explosion. When Laney exploded, she unloaded. Zane's explosions, at least at home, were more like *implosions*. He went silent—something that no one at Bellweather would have predicted. *But we can show up differently in different contexts*, Zane reasoned with himself. *Different relationships call forward different versions of ourselves*. That last thought sounded like it came straight from the mind of Ricardo Bloom, a realization that inclined Zane to resist it.

"The next level up is *subtraction*. At this level, while not necessarily undermining each other, people *resist* each other—each other's ideas, suggestions, help, input, feedback, and so on. This resistance may be obvious, or it may be hidden beneath an outwardly pleasant veneer. *Subtraction*-level relationships are typically characterized by suspicion, wariness, or tension."

Zane glanced across the room at Ricardo and could still feel the tension he felt when Ricardo had turned down his offer without explanation. Ricardo had seemed wary, and Zane had been suspicious of him ever since.

"The next level up is *addition*. At this level, people mostly coexist with others, minding their own business. It's the classic silo situation

LEVELS OF RELATION 57

where individuals, teams, or departments focus on their own work and don't worry so much about what others might be doing. When adding, we may not be making things harder for others by obstructing or resisting them, but we're also not making things easier. Relationships at this level are characterized by a focus on one's own objectives coupled with a relative disinterest in others' goals or perspectives."

Outside of Bellweather's new business, Zane barely focused anymore on the legacy parts of the operation. He supposed that his work relationship with the leaders of those areas was probably at the addition level, which seemed appropriate to him under the circumstances.

"The next level up is *multiplication*," Dot continued. "At this level, as well as focusing on their own work, people actively cooperate and collaborate with others. This cooperation leverages the benefits of mutual helping and accelerates performance beyond simply the summation of separate efforts. Relationships at the multiplication level are characterized by high levels of helpful interaction. The jump to multiplication produces such a leap in productivity that organizations around the world invest heavily into trying to move their people to this level."

We'll get there, Zane assured himself. *Just a few growing pains at the moment.*

"But there's a still higher level of relation that produces much higher gains than even the leap to multiplication. This highest relational level is what we call *compounding*. It is what Teilhard called *convergence*. At this level, people open themselves to each other's goals and realities, integrating them with their own. As a result, other people are no longer 'over there'—separate entities with whom we can cooperate across our divides—but are rather *within* us in meaningful ways. Others and their goals are part of everything we do and every decision we make. Their success becomes as important as our own. Relationships at this level are characterized by high levels of curiosity, consideration, and trust."

Dot turned on the screen and displayed the following . . .

THE LEVELS OF RELATION

2 Compounding
Integrate

1 Multiplication
Collaborate

0 Addition
Coexist

-1 Subtraction
Resist

-2 Division
Obstruct

"These are graphical depictions of these five levels of relation. What similarities and differences do you notice between them?"

After a few moments of silence, Pam raised her hand.

"Yes, Pam, what do you see?"

"Well, to begin with, the numbers are interesting."

"Yes, and do you have an inkling as to why we might have numbered them this way?"

"I suppose it emphasizes how the bottom two levels are truly negative. When we're in relation in those ways, we're actually taking away from and undermining what we otherwise could do together.

"It's interesting that addition only merits a zero, however," she continued. "I would have thought it would register at least in the positive."

Dot nodded. "The zero really means that when we're adding, we aren't adding anything beyond ourselves. We're adding our own efforts to the collective, perhaps even at high levels of competence, and from an individualistic perspective that may seem like a plus. However, the way we're defining *addition* here rates it as a zero relationally, since there is no synergy or upside to us being together. We might just as well work in separate organizations."

"Could I jump in here for a moment?" Ricardo asked. "These relational mathematical titles are interesting in another nonobvious way. Consider a team of five people, with each person showing up and doing their own work at an *addition* level relationally. That would be equivalent to each person bringing a +1 to the sum of the team's efforts, which would yield an output of five for the team. Consider that same five-person team showing up in a relationally *multiplying* way, however. How might the math change in that case?"

"Five times five?" Judy asked.

"As an analogy, yes," Ricardo said. "As we progress relationally together, the improvements are not simply linear. *Multiplication* is not just one point more productive than *addition*, for example. It is *many* times more productive. And *compounding* is still many, many times more productive than that. Mathematically, you might think of it as the difference between $1 + 1 + 1 + 1 + 1$, 5×5, and 5^5, each of which successively yield massively larger numbers. The same could be said in the negative as well: *Subtraction*, in terms of its effect on the group, is way more than one point worse than *addition*, and *division* is many times worse than that. It's a bit like how earthquakes are measured on the Richter scale, where each whole number increase equals a 10-times increase in magnitude."

"You're saying that a five-person organization operating at the *multiplication* level will outproduce an *addition*-level organization by 25 to 5?" Zane asked. "Or that a *compounding* organization will outproduce a *multiplying* organization by 3,125 to 25?"

Ricardo smiled. "That's some quick math, Zane. No, I'm using these numbers only as an analogy. However, each increase in relational level produces a significant and nonlinear jump in organizational performance. I *am* saying that, yes."

"And do you have some proof for that proposition?"

"I would say that your own company's history is rather compelling evidence, Zane. Both positively and negatively."

Zane's smirk disappeared from his face.

There was a time, some 25 years prior, when Bellweather almost went out of business. Zane's father, Frank, in a fit of rage, had dismissed almost his entire executive team, Dot included. Over the next few months, Frank slowly realized what a mistake he had made, as the company was in free fall. Then 30-year-old Dot had acted as a kind of firewall between Frank Savage and the rest of the organization. With that barrier gone, Frank was igniting fires across the company, and people were starting to jump ship. Two of the executives he had fired had joined their chief rival, and the best and brightest at Bellweather were beginning to leave and join them.

This was happening at the same time Frank's family, too, was in crisis. Zane, who had struggled with a drug problem through his teenage years, was locked away in a rehab center, and Frank's wife—Zane's mother—was threatening to leave Frank if he didn't make some drastic changes as a husband and father. The image Frank Savage had tried to cultivate as a successful business- and family-man was unraveling in very public ways. His can-do, forward-marching, military-bred attitude, which had served him so well while building his company, was no longer working. The harder he marched, the more, it seemed, the world resisted.

Nineteen-year-old Zane had hated his father. But now, 44-year-old Zane admired and revered him. During the time Zane was away in therapy, his father had made a sudden shift that both started to heal their own relationship and also won Dot back into his employ. In the years that followed, Bellweather developed into the most widely respected company in their industry. Dot took over as CEO 10 years into that ascent and became not just beloved in the company but revered in the industry at large.

In the rush of these memories, something suddenly struck Zane that had never occurred to him: *He had become his father of 25 years earlier.*

His own marriage, too, was in trouble. His company, despite its incredible legacy and future promise, was, if the numbers Dot and Ricardo were alluding to were true, in some peril, and he was estranged from his oldest child—his son, Jackson. Although Jackson didn't have any substance abuse problems Zane was aware of and was currently attending Stanford, they had barely spoken in six months. In fact, Jackson hadn't even come home over Christmas, electing to take a trip with friends instead. Conversations with him were short, shallow, and somewhat awkward. Zane rubbed his eyes. *My life is like my father's was at its worst point*, he lamented within.

Ricardo's comment that Bellweather's history demonstrated the impact magnitudes of the different levels of relation still hung in the air. "I'll have to think more about that," Zane stammered.

Dot stepped back to the front of the room. "Any additional comments or questions about these levels of relation?" she asked.

"One more if I might," Pam said. "The four lowest levels are similar in that the people are all separated from each other. The separate circles around the people disappear only at the *compounding* level."

"Yes, and what do you think that's getting at, Pam?"

"Well, it's like we drop our barriers at that level. It reminds me of the hydrogen and oxygen atoms example that Ricardo shared. We're open to each other in a way that perhaps we aren't at lower levels."

"Exactly." Dot nodded. "Martin Buber made the same point when he said that at the highest level of relation 'the barriers of the individual are in fact breached and a new phenomenon appears which can appear only in this way: one life open to another.'[18] That's why we show no walls at the *compounding* level of relation.

"We'll get much more into *compounding* as we continue, but for now, and with all of this as background, it's time to build our relational map."

9

Relational Maps

"Go ahead and look at the chart I shared with you earlier," Dot said. "We're now ready to begin populating it. In order to do that, I'd like you to do the following: Rate each of your relationships in this room using the five levels of relation we've been discussing—*division, subtraction, addition, multiplication,* and *compounding.*"

Zane looked around. "But most of us just met. So, in many cases, we barely have a relationship at all."

"Do you know most of the people in your company?" Dot asked.

Zane laughed. "Not at our size now. Not even close."

"Then this room isn't too far off from the reality in many of our workplaces, is it? Not really having a relationship is itself a kind of relationship, and that lack of familiarity is one of the realities that has a bearing on what level of relation we might be experiencing with others. So, take that into account when scoring your relationships in the room.

"Two points of clarification before you all begin, however. First, you are *not* scoring yourself or the other person. Rather, you are scoring the *relationship* between you in terms of the levels of relation we have been discussing. Along your row on the chart, each intersection with the name of someone else in the room represents the relationship between you and that other person. In the square representing each relationship, go ahead and enter a number: -2 for *division*, -1 for *subtraction*, 0 for *addition*, +1 for *multiplication*, or +2 for *compounding*.

"The second point of clarification is that you will score only your own row, which represents the 13 relationships you have in this room. Don't overthink it. Just give an honest assessment of where you think each relationship currently is. Go ahead and begin. We'll take about five minutes for this."

Zane looked down at the chart and began rating the relationships along his row. First up was Judy. He thought about it. Although Judy was on the executive team, he didn't interact much with her. He trusted her to do her job and didn't interfere. He was about to rate the relation at multiplication. However, as he thought further about it, he realized that he didn't really know what she did day to day and didn't know much about her personally. He didn't feel like they got in the way of each other, so the relationship wasn't at -2 or -1. But he couldn't honestly say that they collaborated much either. He scored the relationship at a 0 for *addition*.

Next up was the relationship with Rita. This one was clearly negative. He certainly felt resistant to anything she said, which suggested *subtraction. But did it go even beyond that?* Based on their exchange earlier in the day, she obviously felt that Zane made her work more difficult. As he thought about it, he realized that he felt the same way. Each of them felt undermined by the other. He recorded a -2 for *division*.

Next was Cree. The company wasn't getting what it needed from Cree, and Zane had been figuring out how to replace him. He reasoned that Cree likely felt that he wasn't getting the support he wanted or needed. However, Zane didn't feel like either of them was trying to undermine the other in any way. He actually liked Cree quite a bit, as quirky as he was, but he could feel tension building between them. He went back and forth between -1 and 0 but ultimately rated their work relationship at -1 for *subtraction*.

As he turned to the politicians, he didn't know quite how to think about their relationships. A Republican for most of his life, there was a time when Zane would have automatically reacted negatively to Democrats. But his views had moderated over the years, and he was now a registered Independent. In his position at Bellweather, he also thought it strategically prudent to be politically neutral and to work with leaders of all persuasions to advance the interests of his company and industry. He considered whether any political biases he still carried might color his view of any of the politicians or possible relationships with them, and he honestly didn't think so.

He began thinking of his fledgling relationships with each of them. Of the four, he'd met only Senator Arlo Summers prior to that morning. And although he thought highly of Eliza Schuler and had enjoyed her interesting banter through the day, they really didn't know each other. She'd tweaked him a couple of times, but he didn't believe they were creating problems for each other, and he didn't feel any interior resistance to her. He recorded a 0 for *addition*. The same went for Sam and Dexter, the two Democrats out of the four. In all three of those cases, he wished he could score the relationships higher. Which brought him to Arlo. In Arlo's role as the ranking member on the Armed Services Committee, Zane had twice met with him on the potential security risks posed by quantum computing. Zane found him to be pleasant, straightforward, and serious—more a good accountant than a politician is the line that came to his mind after their first meeting. Zane felt like they were perhaps already at a multiplication level together, so he rated that relationship as a +1.

His relationships with the folks from PERC were easy to grade. Although he had no ill will toward them, he had mostly ignored them so far. Pam had pleasantly surprised him while they were looking at the painting together, but they hadn't really even had a conversation, and he had no real understanding about who they were or what work challenges they faced. He rated all four relationships at the addition level—0.

Which brought Zane to the last two names on the chart: Ricardo and Dot. Zane looked up at Ricardo, who was seated across the room, filling out his own chart. All of their interactions when Zane was recruiting him had felt strained—more like judo matches than real conversations. To Ricardo's credit, he hadn't come off at all that way in the group today, but Zane still harbored frustration. Despite some positive interaction today, he still felt resistant toward him and sensed that Ricardo felt similarly. He rated their relationship at -1 for *subtraction*.

Which brought him to Dot. Zane exhaled and leaned back heavily into his chair. He was suddenly transported in his mind to a scene three years prior.

He and Dot were in the boardroom in the main building on Bellweather's Pittsburgh campus. They had dismissed the board members. It was just the two of them—the sensei and the student, one of them holding a two-of-a-kind in her hand versus the other holding a straight flush. Zane had Dot beat. He had the votes. Which meant he had her job.

"How did we get here, Zane?" she had asked him.

"It's unfortunate," he remembered saying.

"I love this place, you know, like your father did," she had said. "I put my whole professional life into it. I want you to know that my offer still stands. I would be willing to stay on in a kind of elder statesperson role, like your father did. I'm invested in maintaining the culture here, which has been so vital to our success. I could help you with that in the coming years until I retire."

Zane's friend and mentor Hal had been in favor of such an arrangement, and, for an instant, Zane glimpsed some wisdom in it. But he quickly dismissed the idea. So long as Dot was around, everyone would still revere her as the leader, no matter what the titles said to the contrary. They wouldn't look to him. And they wouldn't credit his late father either. They would keep lionizing Dot, and her words and thoughts would continue to drive opinion and strategy. He couldn't allow it.

"You've meant a lot to everyone here, Dot," he told her. "But we're at a point, tough as it may be to hear, that the company needs to grow beyond you."

Zane remembered her silently looking at him for what seemed a full minute. He forced himself not to look away.

"I've known you for a long time, Zane," she finally said. "And it doesn't feel like you're being fully honest with me. I don't think me leaving right now is in the best interest of the company. And I don't think you actually believe that either. That suggests that your insistence that I go is being driven by something else."

Zane bit his lip and shook his head. "It's just your time, Dot," he insisted. "You've made tremendous contributions here, and I'm grateful for all you've done. I know my father was too. But there was a time when he stepped back so that you could step forward. That was the right move then, just as this is the right move now."

Dot looked at him in silence for another moment. "Then we have a problem," she said. "You have the votes to do what you want. But I think you know that I have the people."

Zane tensed up.

"So, if I leave, you will need to do it with honor and dignity."

There it was—the surrender Zane had been hoping for. "Of course!" he had responded overeagerly. "I would never do anything to rob you of your dignity, Dot."

"I'm not talking about *my* dignity, Zane. I'm talking about *yours*. To retain the trust of the workforce, you will need to lead a transition with honor and dignity."

"One more minute!" Dot called out to the group, pulling Zane back to the present. "One more minute to complete your row."

In the intersection of his and Dot's names, Zane entered his final score: -2.

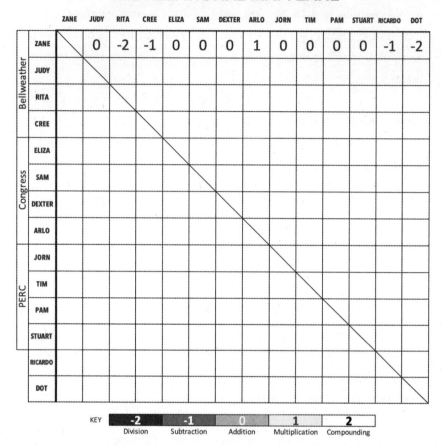

"Okay, everyone, let's now combine and integrate your charts."

Zane hadn't thought about other people looking at his scores. He glanced at the numbers in the spaces for Ricardo and Dot and felt the urge to change them. But the moment passed before he could react. *Oh well, it's honest.*

"We're going to assemble the scores into a grid," Dot said. "It will only take a second. Are there any questions while the data is inputting?"

"Are we going to see each other's scores?" Sam asked.

"Yes. But remember, none of the scores are personal—they're neither scores of other people nor scores of yourselves. They are rather your current evaluations of the collection of *relationships* you have with others in this room. And I think you'll find that the scores you assigned won't be far off from how your colleagues rated them. If any particular relationship score is lower than you'd both like it to be, the thing to start thinking about is how to raise it. As we continue, we'll supply ideas on how to do that."

Pam raised her hand. "Are these scores going to help us build the different kind of org chart that you mentioned earlier?"

"Yes, Pam, exactly. Using your relational scores, we're going to craft a chart that provides visibility into the space—the *between*—on your standard org charts. We call it a *relational map*. It gives a dynamic relational view of an organization—a view of the relational intersections that are actually producing everything for the organization.

"Although we in this room are coming from different organizations, we're going to pretend that we all work in the same company. We'll think of ourselves as being members of the company's executive team, and our relational scores will give us a relational view of that team. In a few minutes, we'll also show you how you can assemble a similar relational chart around the relationships between teams or departments."

Dot turned on the screen again. "Let's take a look at our relational map, shall we? Given the scores you've submitted, this will give us a relational view of our team.

"Every score on the chart is what we call a *relational node*, and together the nodes make up what we call the *relational field* of the team. It's a view of a team that you've probably never had before—not an individual or collective view but a *relational* view.

YOU AND WE

THE RELATIONAL MAP: PEOPLE VIEW

		ZANE	JUDY	RITA	CREE	ELIZA	SAM	DEXTER	ARLO	JORN	TIM	PAM	STUART	RICARDO	DOT	ave
Bellweather (-0.58)	ZANE		0	-2	-1	0	0	0	1	0	0	0	0	-1	-2	-0.38
	JUDY	0		0	-1	0	0	0	-1	0	0	0	0	1	2	0.08
	RITA	-2	0		0	0	0	0	-1	0	0	0	0	0	2	-0.08
	CREE	0	0	-1		0	-1	-1	0	0	0	1	0	0	0	-0.15
Congress (-0.42)	ELIZA	-1	0	0	0		-2	-1	0	0	0	0	0	1	0	-0.23
	SAM	0	0	0	0	-2		1	-1	0	0	0	0	1	1	0.00
	DEXTER	0	0	0	0	0	1		0	0	0	0	0	0	2	0.23
	ARLO	1	0	0	0	-1	-1	1		0	0	0	0	1	1	0.15
PERC (-0.08)	JORN	0	0	0	0	0	-1	0	0		0	1	-1	0	0	-0.08
	TIM	0	0	0	0	1	-1	-1	0	0		0	-1	0	0	-0.15
	PAM	-1	0	1	1	0	1	1	0	0	1		0	1	1	0.46
	STUART	0	0	0	1	1	0	0	1	-1	-1	1		0	0	0.15
	RICARDO	-1	0	0	0	0	0	0	0	0	0	0	0		2	0.08
	DOT	-2	2	1	0	1	1	2	0	0	1	0	0	2		0.62
	ave	-0.46	0.15	-0.08	0.00	0.00	-0.23	0.15	-0.08	-0.08	0.08	0.23	-0.15	0.46	0.69	0.05

KEY:

-2	-1	0	1	2
Division	Subtraction	Addition	Multiplication	Compounding

"Although we're building this relational view for our imaginary team," Dot continued, "we've also put squares around each of the subgroups here—Bellweather, Congress, and PERC. The relational scores inside those boxes will give you a view on the current relational status within your subgroups. The average relational score for each subgroup appears just above the organization's name on the left of the chart."

Zane stared at the results. Nothing higher than addition for his team. Not surprising since he himself scored two of the relationships in the negative. The fact that they scored their relationships even lower than the people from Congress did (-0.58 compared to -0.42) irked him.

He also fixated on three other items on the chart. First, judging from the scores in the last column on the right, he had rated his relationships lower than anyone else had theirs. Second, based on the scores across the bottom, everyone else appeared to have rated their relationships with him more negatively than with anyone else. And finally—and biggest of all for him—Dot had rated their relationship at -2.

The last item wasn't a surprise. Zane had scored it the same way. Dot's score nevertheless popped off the page because theirs was the only relationship she had scored in the negative, much less at -2, and Zane knew everyone else could see it and was thinking about it. He also knew that Dot, who knew very well they would be publishing the results to the group, purposely had not softened the blow.

"So, remember," Dot said, "a score of -2 means *division*, -1 is *subtraction*, 0 is *addition*, +1 is *multiplication*, and +2 is *compounding*. Our average relational score in this room is in the bottom right corner of the chart—0.05. As we sit here, we're just an eyelash's width above *addition* on average."

"Yes, but some are much lower," Eliza observed. "You have to give it up for Zane, coming in at -0.46!"

"That's actually not quite right, Eliza," Dot said. "That number is not a rating of Zane. It's the average of how each of us rated our relationships with Zane. *We* are in that number as much as he is. Me included."

"Yes, from your scores, it looks like y'all have some history."

"We've had some amazing times together," Dot replied. "And, as I'm sure Zane would agree, some rough patches. But again, I was part of those rough patches. That's not just Zane."

"I'm going to bet it was mostly Zane," Eliza drawled.

Something about the way Eliza said that made Zane laugh. She coaxed him to say more, but he knew better and shook his head. However, a faint smile remained.

"One more thing about relational maps," Dot said. "The kind of chart we just built regarding team members can be built, as well, regarding whole teams or departments. And when you build such a chart, you get a relational view of an entire organization. To give you a feel for that,

72 YOU AND WE

I want to show you the same chart we just built but with departmental names in place of your names. Take a look and tell me what it invites you to start thinking about."

THE RELATIONAL MAP: DEPARTMENT VIEW

	MKTG	SALES	OPS	PROD	ENG	MANUF	QUAL	R&D	CUST SERV	STRAT	FIN	LEGAL	HR	IT	ave
MKTG		0	-2	-1	0	0	0	1	0	0	0	0	-1	-2	-0.38
SALES	0		0	-1	0	0	0	-1	0	0	0	0	1	2	0.08
OPS	-2	0		0	0	0	0	-1	0	0	0	0	0	2	-0.08
PROD	0	0	-1		0	-1	-1	0	0	0	1	0	0	0	-0.15
ENG	-1	0	0	0		-2	-1	0	0	0	0	0	1	0	-0.23
MANUF	0	0	0	0	-2		1	-1	0	0	0	0	1	1	0.00
QUAL	0	0	0	0	0	2		0	0	0	0	0	0	2	0.31
R&D	1	0	0	0	-1	-1	1		0	0	0	0	1	1	0.15
CUST SERV	0	0	0	0	0	-1	0	0		0	1	-1	0	0	-0.08
STRAT	0	0	0	0	1	-1	-1	0	0		0	-1	0	0	-0.15
FIN	-1	0	1	1	0	1	1	0	0	1		0	1	1	0.46
LEGAL	0	0	0	1	1	0	0	1	-1	-1	1		0	0	0.15
HR	-1	0	0	0	0	0	0	0	0	0	0	0		2	0.08
IT	-2	2	1	0	1	1	2	0	0	1	0	0	2		0.62
ave	-0.46	0.15	-0.08	0.00	0.00	-0.15	0.15	-0.08	-0.08	0.08	0.23	-0.15	0.46	0.69	**0.05**

KEY	-2	-1	0	1	2
	Division	Subtraction	Addition	Multiplication	Compounding

"Ooh, when you put it in this form, it really gets interesting."

"Why do you say that, Jorn?"

"Well, if I were to apply this to PERC, it gives me an entirely new way of seeing our issues and our opportunities. For example, I can't think of a situation where interdepartmental scores of -1 or -2 are good for the

RELATIONAL MAPS

organization. Those are obvious indications that we need to start working on things cross-functionally. In addition, there are so many zeros on this chart that it illuminates how little lift we are getting across wide swaths of the organization."

"I like how you put that in terms of *lift*, Jorn," Ricardo said from the back of the room. "That's exactly right. Although we are adding inputs to the organization when we're adding, we're not providing lift. That's a great insight."

"I agree," Dot said. "I love that. So here is a question for all of you: If you were leading this company and you had access to this perspective, what would you do next to begin lifting your organization?"

Judy raised her hand. "I think I'd start looking at each of the relational nodes. So, for example, starting on the first row, the marketing–operations relationship is rated at -2 and the marketing–product relationship is rated at -1. I'd ask how important these cross-functional relationships are for the success of the organization. The manufacturing–engineering relationship a few rows down being at -2 is clearly a big problem, and if these other intersections, too, are strategically important, then it would be mission critical to dive into improving them. I hope you're going to give us some tips on how to do that!"

"What if the strategic importance of a given cross-functional relationship isn't very high?" Dot followed up. "What then? Would you ignore it and move on?"

Judy thought about it. "Hmm, maybe if it was *addition*, although Jorn's comment about lack of lift gives me pause. Currently, we might not think that a certain relationship is strategically relevant. But how could we know what could come out of a relationship if they were to climb the ladder toward *compounding*? Whole new business models or processes might emerge in that case. So, our lower relation scores could hold hidden opportunities. Even if not, however, *subtraction* and *division* relationships in an organization are clearly poisonous, as they introduce *drag* into an organization. So, culturally, I don't think we could allow *subtraction* and *division* to continue."

"I'm not sure I agree with that." It was Sam Alton. "In Congress, I need to oppose things I disagree with. In my view, Eliza and Arlo here are trying to push an extreme Republican agenda that I vehemently oppose." He turned to the two of them. "You'd probably say the same about me."

"About your extreme Democratic agenda? Yes."

"So that's my point," Sam continued. "I understand why *multiplication* and *compounding* would be important within our own conferences, but should it also be our goal with members of the other party? That seems like a stretch to me."

Dexter shrugged. "I'm not sure what *multiplying* or *compounding* would look like across the aisle, but I don't think it has to mean helping the other party advance their interests at the expense of our own. I do, however, think that the higher levels of relation would equip us to see more clearly where our interests might align, where we might find compromise, and set us up to do things we couldn't otherwise do."

"It might do even more than that, Dex," Arlo said. "If we remained open to each other in the ways you're describing, maybe we'd discover new possibilities beyond either of our current agendas. Maybe that's what *making water* means in the political arena. You Democrats need to retain your *hydrogen* nature, and we Republicans need to retain our *oxygen* nature, and it's that very difference that might allow for new and better solutions and approaches to emerge. If we can stay open to each other while maintaining that tension, that is."

"That's really sweet, y'all," Eliza chimed in, "but you know as well as I do that voters care more about what we oppose than what we pass. For all the talk of bipartisanship, voters really want us to kick ass. At least, that's what their behavior at the ballot box says."

"That raises a question, doesn't it?" Ricardo asked. "Are you accountable only to those who vote for you or to all the voters in your district?"

"Oh, I'm accountable to all of them—that's why we have a vote. But it's only those who vote for me who keep me in this seat."

"So, what responsibility do you have to people who *don't* vote for you?" Ricardo followed up.

"If I may," Arlo stepped in, "I think we naturally seek to have *multiplication* or *compounding* relationships with people who support and vote for us, partly for the reason you're articulating, Eliza. But, as I think Ricardo is suggesting, wouldn't it be good politics to try to understand *all* the electorate and not just some of it? And aren't we supposed to be representing all of them?"

Eliza didn't respond.

"In fact," Arlo continued, "I think it could be interesting to build one of these relational maps for our communities and for our society as well. What different groups comprise our communities or our society, and then at what levels of relation are the groups operating with each other? That would be really illuminating, I think. It might help us to see possibilities and strategies that we haven't seen before."

"That's a fascinating idea, Arlo," Dot said. "I'd love to see you or someone take a cut at that."

"I think it would be best if it was done in tandem with the people from the various constituent groups. Maybe you could lead something like that on your task force."

"Yes, and maybe you could do it in Congress, too, and we could compare what we're seeing. Let's not forget that idea. Something good might come of it."

Dot looked around at the group. "Really interesting discussion, everyone! But, Eliza, I think you're pointing us toward an important issue. What I hear from you relative to Congress is that even if higher levels of relation among legislators, including colleagues across the aisle, might be a good idea in concept, as a practical matter those efforts aren't currently rewarded, which disincentivizes any such effort. Is that capturing what you're thinking about, at least in part?"

"Yeah, it is. I'm not going to be a Pollyanna. In a way, I hate myself for saying it, but it's the truth."

Dot nodded. "It's not only a political issue. There are realities in every organization that invite higher levels of relation and others that incentivize and reward lower levels. Leaders who understand how their collective results are driven by relation locate and replace elements that increase relational drag in their organizations with elements that increase relational lift."

Zane looked down at the chart in his lap. The relational scores with and between his own team members were abysmal. *But there is much more to leadership than that!* he reasoned. *My dad built up a whole company despite having the relational abilities of a rock. Yes,* he argued with himself, *but the company almost disintegrated because of it and only survived when he finally saw what he had been doing to everyone.*

"To lead well," Dot continued, "you need sightlines into the elements that both impede and promote relation. We want to share with you an approach that will provide that kind of visibility—a lens that equips you to see groups and organizations in four dimensions. We call it *the 4-Dimensional Playing Field*."

10

The 4-Dimensional Playing Field

To introduce this way of seeing organizations," Dot said, "pick an organizational problem, and let's think about it together. Go ahead and shout something out."

"Lack of accountability," Jorn called out.

"Okay, and what does that look like, Jorn?"

"People don't do what they say they'll do."

Dot entered his response into her tablet.

"Great. What else does poor accountability look like?"

"A lot of blaming of others," Rita said.

"Not owning up when things go wrong," Eliza added.

"Great," Dot said. "And what kinds of attitudes do you see that correlate with poor accountability?"

"Entitlement."

"Laziness."

"Lack of initiative."

78　　　　　　　　　　YOU AND WE

She recorded these responses as well.

"Can you think of organizational systems, processes, or structures that might undercut or disincentivize accountability?" she asked.

The group thought about it for a moment.

"Top-down management," Rita said.

"Lack of role clarity," Judy added.

"A broken performance management system," Pam said.

"Okay, terrific. How about community or cultural elements that might encourage or incentivize lack of accountability?"

"A no-mistakes culture," Judy answered.

"Or maybe the opposite—a laissez-faire one," Pam said.

"How about lack of real community?" Arlo added.

"Okay, very good," Dot said. "You've identified different dimensions of the problem of lack of accountability. You've shared *behavioral* aspects of the problem, *attitudinal* facets of the problem, *structural* conditions that add to the problem, and *community* features of the problem. These four dimensions—*behavior, attitude, structure,* and *community*—form what I think of as the playing field of every organization, whether family, company, or society.[19]

"The first two dimensions—*behavior* and *attitude*—apply to the individuals in the organization. The last two dimensions—*structure* and *community*—apply to the group or collective.

"Cut a different way, two of the dimensions, *behavior* and *structure*, refer to things you can see, measure, or touch. You might think of these as the *outer* dimensions. The other two dimensions, *attitude* and *community*, refer to the inner states of individuals and the group—things you can feel but not see. You might think of these as the *inner* dimensions.

"These two sets of distinctions—*individual* versus *group* on the one hand and *outer* versus *inner* on the other—give us a four-dimensional view of any group or organization. Let me show you what I mean, using the issue of lack of accountability as a specific example." Dot then shared the following diagram on the screen . . .

A 4-DIMENSIONAL VIEW OF ORGANIZATIONS AND THEIR ISSUES

(lack of accountability as an example)

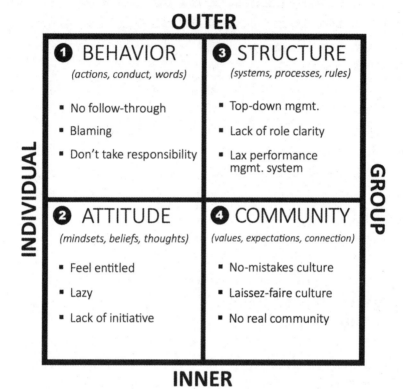

"What about culture?" Pam asked. "Does that fit here somewhere?"

"Good question, Pam. We used to use the word *culture* in place of *community*. But we ended up opting for *community* because the term *culture* is used so often and in different ways that, unless it is defined clearly and understood in the same way by everyone, it ends up meaning everything and therefore nothing. Having said that, if you'd like, you could think of culture this way: All four quadrants together generate the culture of a collective. In that respect, *culture* is a word we can use to express the totality of the quadrants. Does that make sense?"

"Yes, thank you."

"Now, let's think a bit more about these four dimensions or quadrants," Dot continued. "To begin with, which of them would you say is most important for organizational success? We'll go one quadrant at a time. Raise your hand if you would say that *behavior* is the most important."

Three people raised their hands, all three of them from PERC—Jorn, Tim, and Stuart.

"Okay, the PERC team feels pretty strongly about this! Why do you think the behavior quadrant is most important?"

"Because, at the end of the day, mission success depends on what you do or don't do," Jorn said. "If you change people's beliefs but their behaviors don't change, that's no change at all."

"Okay, great, thank you. How about *attitude*? Who believes that attitude is the most important quadrant?"

Zane, Dexter, and Arlo raised their hands.

"Great, and why?"

"You and I used to talk about this at Bellweather," Zane said. "You won't get the behaviors you want if the mentalities or mindsets aren't right. Everything starts with that."

"That's certainly what I used to believe, Zane. But I don't think it's quite that simple anymore. We'll get to that in a bit. How about the rest of you? Why is *attitude* the most important quadrant from your point of view?"

"For me, it's more about the importance of being real with people," Dexter said. "If others don't feel that you care about them, it won't much matter what you do or say—they'll be skeptical."

"Do you have an example of that?" Dot asked.

"In politics, it's an everyday thing. Voters have to feel like you care about them. Which means that you either need to actually care about them or you need to get really good at faking that you do. Since I'm not smart enough to fake people out, I think you just need to keep it real. Same holds true when working on legislation. The Republicans, led by

THE 4-DIMENSIONAL PLAYING FIELD

Arlo here, in fact, had been trying to push a crime reform bill for years. That thing was dead at least 20 times, but Arlo kept talking about it and bringing it forward. He was never angry about it, he didn't posture, he didn't go around trying to use it to score political points. And, over time, I and others on my side of the aisle could tell that this was something that he really cared about and believed in, and when the politics shifted just enough, we started opening up to consider it. Eventually, after a lot of bipartisan work, we ended up passing a bill. But I don't think any of that would have happened without Arlo just being a real person about it."

"Then why did you put a 0 on our relationship?" Arlo laughed. "I at least put it at a 1!"

"I couldn't overlook all the other battle scars!"

Arlo smiled. "I get it, believe me."

"Thanks to both of you for sharing," Dot said. "Okay, next quadrant: Who would rank *structure* as the most important?"

Judy, Cree, and Eliza raised their hands.

"Okay, why?"

"This is the part, for me, that makes things really difficult in the political arena," Eliza said. "It's like Dex was just sayin'. That crime bill passed—yes, in part because Arlo and others didn't weaponize it politically—but especially because the political interests of both parties happened to align around it within the same time frame. Those were structural happenstances, and I'm sorry to say that the structures, systems, and processes of our political system don't usually incentivize and reward that kind of bipartisan cooperation. If you don't establish structures and processes that incentivize bipartisanship, you're not going to like the behaviors and attitudes that politicians end up displaying. Gosh, *we* don't even like it half the time. Am I right?" Eliza looked around for confirmation from her colleagues, who all nodded. "You can preach good attitudes and helpful behaviors all you want, but if the system rewards you for something different, that 'something different' is going to win."

"It's the same in business," Cree agreed. "I run the engineering department at Bellweather, and the behaviors and attitudes of my team are affected more by system and process requirements than by anything else. Zane may think he's running the company, but we're ruled mostly by the requirements we exist within. It's like the Deep State of the company."

Zane rolled his eyes. *Deep State? Really, Cree?*

"These are all compelling cases," Dot said. "Thank you.

"Finally, who thinks *community* is the most important quadrant?"

Pam, Rita, and Sam raised their hands.

"Make your case."

"Well, I think there are a number of things related to community that are critical for organizations," Rita said. "First of all, a unifying and motivating purpose or mission is critically important—something distinctive and meaningful that everyone can own and rally around. Psychological safety is critically important to company success as well, as is a sense of belonging."

"Along those lines," Sam said, "I would add that a strong sense of community is what keeps you bound together during hard times and challenges. It's what makes a group resilient. Without it, you splinter into self-interested groups when the pressure heats up. Which, on the Hill, is often."

"Well, you've all made good arguments in favor of each of the quadrants," Dot remarked. "So, what's the verdict? Which quadrant is most important?"

"I'm not sure you can choose," Pam replied. "It's like saying the best way to make your bed is to pull on one corner of the sheet. You need all four corners to make the bed. I think it's likely the same for organizations."

"That's a brilliant analogy, Pam. Thank you! And notice from what you've said that each of the quadrants affects the others. Attitudes affect behaviors. But behaviors affect attitudes as well—other people's behaviors and our own. Studies show, for example, that posed smiling has a significant impact on attitude.[20] And a dopamine rush from exercise certainly affects one's mood! Attitudes are also profoundly affected, as Eliza and Cree said, by structural issues and, as Rita and Sam argued, by the level of community in the culture of an organization."

"But I could argue all of those in the reverse as well—that attitude affects all the other quadrants," Zane countered.

"Yes, Zane, exactly. Which means we agree that realities in every quadrant affect each of the other quadrants. No one quadrant is fundamental. Each is part of an integrated puzzle—the outer and inner parts of both *me* and *us*.

"The analyses we do of organizations at the task force is four-dimensional. We measure the degree to which realities in each of the four quadrants in organizations are either promoting or undercutting productive work relationships and connectivity. The analysis produces an overall score on the -2 to +2 scale, which is made up of the scores in each of the four quadrants. For ease of digesting the data, we've used a -200 to +200 scale to get rid of decimal points. A score toward -200 in a quadrant indicates *division*, -100 indicates *subtraction*, 0 indicates *addition*, +100 indicates *multiplication*, and +200 indicates *compounding*. You all are here because, although as a society we can't afford for you to fail, you are currently scoring significantly in the negative."

"Can we see our numbers?"

"Yes, Jorn. You're now prepared to understand them. We'll distribute only your own organization's scores to you, however. It's up to you whether you want to share your results with others."

Dot and Ricardo began distributing reports to each of the people in the room. "The numbers might tell a story," Dot said, as she handed Zane the results.

He looked down at Bellweather's scorecard.

YOU AND WE

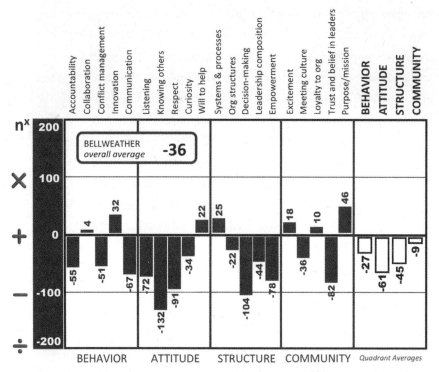

He studied it for a minute to make sure he understood what it was saying. Their overall score was -36—well below *addition* and a third of the way toward full-on *subtraction*. He frowned and shook his head. They scored in the negative in all the quadrants, although just barely in the *community* quadrant. He did a double take when he noticed that their lowest quadrant was *attitude*. *How can that be?* he wondered. *We invest heavily there.* It didn't make sense. And then he noticed the note at the bottom of the chart, disclosing how people at different levels scored the company. Senior leaders experienced Bellweather at a +35 level, directors at a +3 level, managers at a -76 level, and individual contributors at a -31 level.

Zane rested the report on his lap, closed his eyes, and took a deep breath. *How could things be going so poorly when the company is finally making the moves that will catapult us to a whole new level? Clearly,*

THE 4-DIMENSIONAL PLAYING FIELD

managers and individual contributors are feeling disconnected from what we're doing. Maybe I miscalculated by not involving more people in the strategic planning process. Maybe it was a mistake to keep everything under wraps. Maybe we should have been communicating our plans all along. He looked at the sheet again. *I thought the directors knew and understood, but their scores indicate a gap there too.*

"Okay, everyone," Dot called to the group. "I'd like you to gather with your colleagues of your respective organizations and discuss what you're seeing in the numbers. By the way, you'll see that we scored five key elements in each quadrant. Do the numbers support what you are seeing in your organization? Are there surprises? How do you make sense of the results? Let's take 15 minutes for that and then gather back."

The Bellweather team gathered to the far corner of the room, against the window looking out over the Glenstone grounds. "So, what do you think of the report?" Zane asked, not wanting to go first.

"It's interesting," Judy responded.

"How so?"

"Two things jump out at me. The first is, we don't know each other. Look at our score on that element: -132! I don't even know how that's possible, it's so bad. I think it reflects how siloed we've become. And it's only going to get worse as we've almost doubled our remote workforce since moving to DC. The second issue that jumps out at me from the scores is that we have a leadership problem."

"Why do you say that?" Zane asked. "The senior leaders score the company quite a bit better than the rest of the people do because we see and know things that they don't. It looks to me that we actually have a manager problem."

"That's how you're reading that difference?" Rita asked. "You think the people lower in the company submitted poor ratings because they are just blind or ignorant? What if it's exactly the other way around—that people at those levels see and know things that people at the top don't? Maybe it's you and the rest of the people in the C-suite who are blind or ignorant."

Cree cut in with a comment. "Look at how low the company scores in *trust* and *belief in leaders*. Is that what you're referring to, Rita?"

The question broke Rita away from her focus on Zane. "Yes, well, partly, Cree. You can actually see it in scores across the board. People don't feel empowered—that element scores at -78. And they aren't feeling respected either, which scores at -91. And it looks like people don't feel listened to, scoring at -72, which might be why they don't feel respected. These kinds of scores are not symptoms of blindness. They're the kinds of scores people give when they feel like things they are seeing and saying are being ignored. Which is why I would say that the ignorance that is threatening the company is not ignorance at the bottom but ignorance at the top."

"Those are interesting observations, Rita," Judy said.

For his part, Zane was reeling. He wanted to push back against what Rita had said and searched the report for evidence that could be used in his favor. He fixated on the score for *purpose and mission*—which, after all, was what he'd been focusing so heavily on. It was their highest score. By a lot. He took some solace in that. But the score was just 46—so, less than halfway from *addition* to *multiplication*. It looked good only in comparison to all the other scores. And despite the emphasis they had long placed on mindset change and the structural changes they had been making over the prior couple of years, *attitude* and *structure* were their lowest scoring quadrants. He shook his head. *It can't be right*, he argued within. *All our efforts can't be making matters worse.*

Judy reached out and touched his shoulder. "How are you doing, Boss?"

"Who are you asking—me, or the rest of the people in the company?"

"I'm asking you, the person that people at Bellweather believed in enough to follow to DC, even if it meant uprooting their lives and families to do so."

"Because they still believe in the mission," Zane said.

"Yes, and in the person who feels that mission more deeply than any of us."

Zane raised his head and looked at her.

"Look, the numbers aren't good," she said. "But the assessment didn't ask every question that could have been asked, and it didn't probe every issue. If Zane Savage had been on the assessment, I guarantee you the numbers would be higher in support of him than you might be thinking in this moment. You're a force, Zane. It's just that I think people are communicating that they'd like to add their forces to yours. That's what I'm taking from this. This isn't a vote against Bellweather or against you. It's a huge hand in the air saying they currently don't feel like an integrated part of it and want to be involved—more involved than they've been. And that's a positive message."

"I agree with that," Rita said. "That's certainly what I've wanted. Still do, in fact. I want to bring more to my job than I feel I've been allowed to bring. I want to feel like Bellweather is about *us*, all of us—that it's *our* mission, and that we're involved in influencing and co-creating the future of the company."

But I thought we have *been involving everyone,* Zane thought to himself. *At least to an appropriate degree. Have I ever said anything to the contrary?* He looked out the window across the Glenstone grounds, and for a moment his mind wandered far away from the room and from Bellweather. *How would my family score on this assessment?* He could guess the answer. *I wonder how Laney's been doing.* He pushed that thought away only to have it replaced by another.

Maybe it's time to call Jackson.

11

Divides and Differences

Okay, everyone, let's pull back together. How were your discussions in your teams?"

"Good."

"How so, Rita?"

"The results gave us a window into issues we haven't been addressing. It's clear that people in our company aren't feeling listened to or valued. We have lots of walls and divides across the company."

"What do you think you need to do about that?"

"I'm hoping you can tell us."

Dot smiled and nodded. "How about the rest of you? What came up in your discussions?"

"Regarding walls," Jorn said, "we figured that if an organization's silos aren't fighting against or resisting each other, they'll probably end up around 0 on this scale—or the *addition* level of relation. However, if the silos resist or go after each other, the numbers go increasingly negative."

"That's what we see in our group," Dexter said. "Some of our numbers, frankly, aren't as bad as I was expecting. But that's because you have two parts in the organization that more or less hang together—Republicans with Republicans and Democrats with Democrats. It's not quite so simple as that, of course, as both parties have serious and sometimes bitter differences of opinion within their own ranks, but it roughly holds true. If you broke the numbers out by group, I'd expect that some of the numbers inside our own party conferences would be higher, while the numbers across conferences would be far more negative."

"We have those numbers for you, Dex, if you want them. And yes, you're right, although we do see divides within each of your conferences as well. One of the characteristics of siloed organizations is that in-group levels of relation are typically better than out-group levels of relation. *Us-them* lines are a real thing. They carve up organizations just like they carve up societies.

"Consider the lines in this room. In this small group, we have lines between companies, political parties, leadership levels, racial backgrounds, religious affiliations, sexual orientations, and so on. All of these and other lines exist within organizations. Here are a few such lines." She then showed the following on the screen . . .

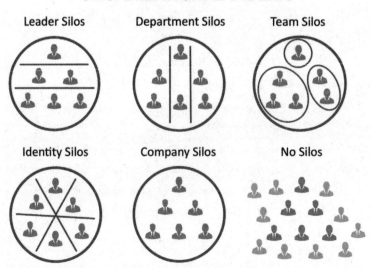

DIVIDES AND DIFFERENCES 91

"Do you see any of these in your organizations?"

Most nodded.

"It's helpful to remember that we weren't born with lines. We've learned to draw them. I remember my father telling me that 'Kesslers don't do that.' Which meant that non-Kesslers do. And voilà, the world was suddenly split between Kesslers and non-Kesslers, with the implication that Kesslers were somehow better."

"Dot, can I add something here?" Ricardo asked.

"Yes, Ricardo. Please."

Turning to the group, he said, "It's important to realize that the very lines we draw reinforce rather than undercut our relationality. Difference only exists in relation. Any conception of a *self*, for example, necessarily designates a *not-self*. *I* and *other* come into existence together. Which is to say that the idea of *I* makes sense only in the context of a *you*, and *Kessler* exists as a surname only in a world that contains *not-Kesslers*! Which means that the boundaries we draw around and between us don't really need to divide us. Rather, they are the places where we are defining ourselves in relation to each other.

"So, the question of where and how we draw our lines is a vital one, as those same lines *can* become battle lines. Let's begin with the most basic line we draw and the line that lies behind every other one: the line between *me* and *you*. A common place to draw this line is at the boundary of one's body. From this point of view, the body and everything inside it is *me*, and everything outside the body is *not-me*. Make sense?"

Most in the room nodded.

"This seems a perfectly reasonable place to draw our boundary," he said. "After all, our bodies do have verifiably separate spatial locations! However, many if not most of us actually draw the *me/not-me* line in a different place. To see how that's the case, I want to ask all of you a question: Do you experience yourself as *being* a body or as *having* a body?"

"*Having* a body," Judy answered.

"Is it the same for most of the rest of you? Not sure? Well, to the extent you think or speak of *having* or *possessing* your body, you have experientially placed your body on the other side of the line. You identify it as *yours* but not as *you*. This rendition of the *me/other* line is woven into the very fabric of the modern Western world. With his famous words, 'I think therefore I am,' the father of modern philosophy, René Descartes, divided the world into billions of pieces by drawing a line around every individual human mind. This is the *me/other* line location that has come to dominate human self-conception in the Western world over the last few centuries.

"But that's not the end of the story. We often draw an even more restrictive line than Descartes. Have you ever, for example, felt ashamed of some thoughts you've had or things you've done and come to think of them as being simply aberrations of yourself—that is, as *not-self*, or not really you?"

Zane's outbursts toward Laney leaped to his mind, as did the silent treatment that was hardening into estrangement from his son, Jackson.

"This is a way of carving the *me/not-me* line through the middle of one's psyche," Ricardo continued, "so that a certain portion of ourselves that we approve of—let's call it the *persona*—is experienced as the real self while the unsavory inclinations in the ego are banished to the *not-self* territory that needs to be controlled or hidden. Carl Jung called these unwanted attributes that we push into our subconscious the *shadow*, where they do damage below the surface of our awareness.

"Although there are many different kinds of psychological therapies, most approaches try to sew the divided parts of a self together again—to reconcile the persona with the other parts of us.[21] Growth and healing come as a person learns to expand her identity by moving the line further and further out and including more of the formerly excluded territory as part of her identity. Line contraction is the malady; expansion is the cure.

"Which raises a fascinating and important possibility: Might the cure for the malady of organizational and societal fracturing lie, as well, in the direction of expansion? I think we all experience something in our lives that suggests this might be the case. Think about someone you love. Maybe it's a partner, a child, or a friend. For me, I'm thinking about what I felt when each of my children were born: I loved them instantly, to the extent that I knew I would lay down my life for them

DIVIDES AND DIFFERENCES 93

without thinking twice. I don't know how best to capture this new feeling and conviction except to say that my heart expanded: My concerns expanded, my awareness expanded, my thoughts expanded, my feelings expanded. I somehow grew larger."

Zane thought back to the moment that Jackson was born. It had been a hard labor for Laney—nearly 24 hours. And then, finally, with a last, exhausting push, Jackson appeared. He was a deep shade of ashen gray. And he wasn't breathing. The nurses rushed him away without comment, and Zane remembered collapsing into a chair. It had never struck him until that moment that he didn't even go to Laney to comfort her. He just folded into himself, numb and empty.

Then, 30 seconds or so later, he heard a baby's gasping cry from across the hallway, and a few moments after that, the nurses reentered the room and laid Jackson on Laney's breast. They had both broken down in tears of joy and relief, and Zane remembered the thought that came to him at that moment: *I'll do anything for this boy. Anything.*

"One way to make sense of this," Ricardo continued, "is to say that my *I/other* line expanded—that is, the circumference of how I defined and experienced myself expanded to include my children. My identity grew—my *heart* expanded, if you will. It grew beyond a separate me, which was always just an abstraction anyway, and it can continue to grow. So, for example, I can expand from caring only about myself, to caring about those who are like me, which is what happened as I felt myself expanding to include my children. But I can expand still further. I can begin to care about and feel compassion for those who are unlike me, and then those who don't like me, and then even those who oppose me. And so on. Our hearts can expand. We can become larger."

Zane was transported back two weeks to an interaction he and Laney had when she had come back to their place in Alexandria to grab some things—items Zane had refused to take to her.

Zane remained lying on the couch in the living room reading a book as she was packing. The silence in the home pressed down on him in metric tons. He kept reading and rereading the same page. His heart raced, and he was careful even to swallow quietly, to appear as nonchalant and unmoved as possible. "You want to get off your butt and help me with this?" Laney had said, trying to carry a large box down the stairs. Without a word, Zane placed his book on the floor and slowly got up from the couch. He labored up the staircase, turned his back to Laney, and, with his hands behind him, grabbed one end of the box and began walking down the stairs. "Not so fast! Jeez!" she said. Zane slowed. "But don't stop! Keep going."

"It's always something, isn't it?" Zane had said in practiced calm.

"Oh, go to hell, Zane. You don't care about anything or anyone but yourself."

"I'm helping *you*, aren't I?"

"Yeah, I suppose this is about what help looks like to you."

Zane didn't say anything more, and he had congratulated himself on keeping his cool despite the provocations.

And yet, listening to Ricardo speak, Laney's words kept ringing in his ears. *"You don't care about anything or anyone but yourself."*

"As our lines expand and our identities grow, so do our perspectives," Ricardo continued. "Evolutionarily speaking, humankind's development has been in terms of the very expansion of experienced identities we are discussing—at both the individual and group levels. The group-level equivalent of the *me/other* line is the *us/them* line. These are the lines on which battles are fought, and the wars of history have been waged. As human beings evolved together, one of the key markers of development was that this line got pushed progressively further out, so that people increasingly began to see more people as part of them rather than outside of or against them. Family identities expanded to tribal identities, which expanded to inter-tribal identities, which expanded to various levels beyond—to nation-state levels of identity, and so on. Each successive level maintained the combinations that had previously converged and added additional combinations to the group, so that human development has been characterized by the emergence of ever more inclusive *attitudes, behaviors, communities,* and *structures.*

DIVIDES AND DIFFERENCES

"Our advancement as a species has been for exactly this reason—our ability to expand and include more within our group. This ability to expand is our most uniquely human trait—the trait, more than any other, that has enabled Homo sapiens to do what no other species have done. Both for good and for ill, I might add."

Sam raised his hand. "What if I disagree with another person or group? Are you suggesting we should nevertheless expand to include them in that case? If so, I'm not sure I can go there. For example, if I'm being honest, I think the Republican agenda will set our country back 50 years to a bygone time that might have been wonderful for some segment of the population but was terribly oppressive for many others."

"And I think the Democratic agenda will enslave us to a massive federal bureaucracy and replace traditional and proven moral values with a leftist woke agenda," Eliza shot back. "If I'm being honest."

"Well, we certainly have a line here, don't we!" Dot said.

"More like a moat," Dexter replied.

Dot stepped back to the front of the room. "Let me ask all of you something. Ricardo shared that he felt his soul expanding to include his children. Do you think that means that he now gives them everything they want? That he agrees with everything they do? That he won't correct them if he thinks they're on the wrong track?"

People around the room shook their heads.

Dot looked at Ricardo for a response. "Certainly not!" he said.

"So, does an expansive identity—feeling care and compassion, as Ricardo put it—mean that I approve of or condone whatever they say or do? That I give up my own convictions? That I avoid conflict and roll over?"

"No," Pam answered. "Because you want to make water, and the only way you can do that is if hydrogen stays hydrogen and oxygen stays oxygen. You have to embrace your difference."

"Yes, Pam—while?"

"While—well, while still staying open to the other, I suppose?"

"Yes, exactly," Dot said. "Hydrogen must have enough respect for oxygen, and vice versa, that they're willing to hold tightly to each other and each other's differences. That's the only way to create a future that doesn't just devolve into a battle for a world that is composed only of either hydrogen or oxygen. You must believe enough in your own views still to hold to them, while also being humble enough to recognize that we need a world bigger and better than what I and my kind alone can imagine—or, for that matter, what you and your kind can dream up. We want water, and no *one* side can discover and create that alone.

"One of the things that's misunderstood about relation," she continued, "is the importance of *difference*. Ricardo mentioned this earlier, but I want to reemphasize it. Think about it: The direction north, for example, has meaning only in relation with south, and the relation between them is what brings both north and south into being. There *is* no north without south. Pick your category—relation with difference is what brings everything into being: mother and child, leader and follower, speaker and listener, buyer and seller, Republican and Democrat. And it is out of these differences that the new emerges."

"Can I build on that a little?" Ricardo asked.

"Of course, please."

He stepped to the front of the room again. "On this point about difference, I'd like to share just a tiny bit of philosophy with all of you."

"Why did I know you were going to say something like that?" Eliza said, rolling her eyes.

Ricardo laughed. "Don't feel intimidated or turned off by it. I'm not a philosopher myself, but even *I* find what I'm about to share with you interesting."

"That's not particularly reassuring," Eliza deadpanned.

"Probably not," Ricardo said, still chuckling. "But I'm going to bet that this will interest you, too, Eliza."

"Why do you think that?"

"Because I believe it will illuminate what is currently troubling you about your job."

12

Hegel's Spiral

Two centuries ago," Ricardo began, "an important German philosopher named Georg Wilhelm Friedrich Hegel began analyzing the development of thought and history through a powerful lens—how history and thought emerge through the relational interplay of the kinds of differences we have been discussing.

"Among other things, his work shows how we help to create much of our own opposition—how far-left Democrats help to create and therefore elect far-right Republicans and vice versa, for example, how harried parents invite rebellious kids and vice versa, and how hard-charging corporate leaders produce unengaged workforces and vice versa. Think of any person or group you feel yourself resisting. I'm suggesting that you are helping to maintain that group exactly as they are. Which probably sounds crazy."

"Yes, it does," Zane replied, thinking of Laney.

"I invite you to withhold judgment for now just in case there might be some merit to the claim. After all, if true—that is, if we actually *do* help to create our problems and even our enemies—then perhaps there is something we can do to *stop* creating them."

"So, you're saying that if someone mistreats you it's your own fault?" Rita asked.

Ricardo paused. He grabbed a chair that had been resting against the wall behind him and sat down. "Thank you for raising that, Rita. You are reminding me to slow down and to choose my words more carefully and considerately. No, I'm not saying that. And neither, I believe, was Hegel. Acts of unprovoked and uninvited inconsideration and even violence are devastating and heartbreaking features of most of our lives. I've known my share of it myself. And I'm willing to bet that most of us in the room have. You probably have, too, maybe even in crushing ways."

Rita's gaze dropped to her lap.

Ricardo paused again and silently looked around the room. "My heart goes out to you—to all of you—for the pains you are silently carrying. Victims are not to blame for the aggressions of their abusers, nor for the existence of those abusers. Some people will choose to oppose us regardless of what we do, and some will mistreat us because of demons they themselves are dealing with."

His eyes met Rita's, who silently nodded and responded to his warm gaze with a faint smile. "I'm sorry, Rita. It was not my intent to bring up painful memories."

"No, it's all right," she said. "But thank you. I felt that was an important issue to raise."

"*Very* important," he said. "Thank you for inviting me to slow down to consider and acknowledge it."

He slowly stood back up, and then said, "Again, there are situations characterized by abuse that lie outside of what we're discussing. However, in other parts of our lives, far from the territories of such abuses, it's worth considering how we might be helping to create and sustain more of the resistance around us than we realize. To a surprising degree, the forces we feel opposing us can be our own co-creations."

"How?" Eliza asked.

"Hegel theorized that all of history develops through an interplay of co-created opposites—one idea or position giving rise to competing or oppositional thoughts and positions, which then force a further evolution beyond any of those thoughts or positions, and so on.

"If you look around, you will see this pattern everywhere. Consider, for example, what might seem like a run-of-the-mill situation at work. An employee I will call John pitches an idea in a team meeting. He's convinced about a certain product strategy and is trying to get the team to agree. His colleague Amy feels uneasy about John's plan. As she thinks things through, she believes she has a better idea and pitches it in the next meeting.

"From a Hegelian point of view, even if Amy's idea is completely different from John's, his idea nevertheless is partly responsible for Amy's. Why? Because Amy wouldn't have thought of or so strongly advocated for her idea had John not first pitched his. Her reaction was a response to his action. This co-creative reality is communicated by the words themselves: Every *re*action is, by definition, a response to a prior action."

"Like tic-tac-toe," Eliza said with a grin.

"Exactly." Ricardo smiled and nodded. "And when considered in this way, we can see the co-creative, co-constitutive reality of many things that before seemed separate. We are always in others' responses to us, which means that we may actually be inviting many of the things in others that we blame them for. This doesn't remove responsibility from the people who are responding to us, as they still choose the nature of their responses. But they are responding to their experience with *us*, which means that, like it or not, we are inside those responses in some form or fashion far more often, and more prominently, than we may suppose."

Zane thought about Ricardo's rejection of his pitches to join Bellweather. *Was I in his response? Was his rejection something we produced together?* He thought about it. *But how? I came with an incredible offer.*

Then his thoughts turned to Laney. She had been threatening to leave him for years, but he'd turned himself off from even caring. The linkage between her wanting to leave and him not caring was suddenly obvious to him, in both directions. *How can you let yourself care about someone who wants to leave you? And, on the other hand, why would you ever want to stay with someone who didn't care?*

He relived the moment he discovered that she'd left. He had returned home from a short business trip to find that her side of their closet had been cleared out. No note. No message. No call. Just an empty closet. Looking into that emptiness, an aching pain gripped Zane's chest, from his heart to his navel. He felt like he'd been ripped open, and he staggered to the bathroom counter to keep himself from collapsing. *I always cared*, he cried out within as he relived the scene. *But how would she have known?* asked another voice.

"Many who have grappled with Hegel's work, and it's a slog to be sure," Ricardo continued, "summarize part of that work with three words Hegel himself never used but that simplify what he was describing. Here is how it goes: Any stated idea, action, or cultural or structural reality is a *thesis*. Others then respond with ideas and solutions they like better. Any such response to a thesis is an *antithesis*. Just as a *reaction* is co-created with the prior *action*, an *antithesis* owes its existence, in part, to the *thesis* in response to which it was birthed. *Theses* and *antitheses* inherently compete, and out of the tension of their differences, a new higher-order resolution may eventually be reached. This higher order resolution is a *synthesis*.

"According to Hegel, this repeating dialectic is the pattern of all development and history.[22] Every action invites a reaction, which forces a higher-order resolution, which then sparks its own reaction, and so on. *Thesis, antithesis, synthesis.* Onward and hopefully upward. It's what I call *Hegel's Spiral*. Here is a simple diagram of this pattern.

HEGEL'S SPIRAL

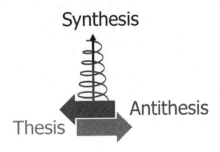

"The theory posits that development unfolds in this order. But is that necessarily true? History certainly reaffirms Hegel's Spiral, over and over. But is that the only possible pattern available to history, or to the present? Do organizations inexorably leap from *thesis* to *antithesis* to *synthesis* in an ongoing spiral, or is another pattern of development available to us? Does the same spiral dictate what will unfold in our homes, or on the streets of our communities as well? Or might there be other possibilities?"

"That's pretty much the picture of legislation," Dexter said. "One side pushes a bill, the other party resists it and pushes their own version, and then, sometimes, we reach an agreement—a *synthesis* bill, if you will. Like the crime bill I mentioned that Arlo led out on."

"With all due respect, Dex, I don't think that's at all what it usually looks like," Eliza disagreed. "While it's true that one side often pushes a bill that the other side resists, on most issues I don't think we're looking for synthesis at all. Rather, we push bills we favor when it seems our own party has the leverage and power to push it through ourselves, the other side be damned. And when we know we don't have the power to get our ideas passed, we don't bring them forward. Look at the record—whether on health care, immigration, the environment, you name it. If one party is in the majority, they try to cram through their own agenda, and the minority party tries to stop it. Neither party wants to give the other any political wins, so compromise is often viewed as weakness—as sacrificing one's values. Neither we nor our constituents want synthesis in those cases."

"So, you prefer gridlock," Zane said.

"We wouldn't put it that way, no," she said. "But I understand if that's what it looks like."

"It does. And you could never run a company that way."

"Can't you?" Dot asked. "I rather think that's how companies are often run."

"By gridlock?" Zane asked incredulously.

"No, by what is *causing* the gridlock: an unwillingness to value or consider ideas different from one's own. One approach—the one Eliza was just describing—is that there is one correct perspective. It might be my own party's perspective, for example, or that of a certain corporate, religious, or other leader. I call this the *Dominator View.* Dominators want to subdue all other viewpoints and win them to their own—by, as Martin Buber said, *injecting their "rightness" into others.*[23] They believe the world will be better as it falls more in line with their own enlightened perspective.

"A very different viewpoint, and one that values synthesis, is that the arc of progress is in the direction of new and higher-order perspectives. According to this view, the world progresses as differing perspectives mix and merge and lift older perspectives, including one's own, to new forms and heights. I call this the *Emergent View.*[24] Emergents try to expand their circles of exposure to include more perspectives. Their goal is not victory but growth and discovery. They believe in a better future than even their own current perspectives can conceive or deliver. Not only do they not feel threatened by synthesis, they try to *start* with synthesis as often as possible—by searching out and trying to understand as many different perspectives as they can, even in advance of acting."

"What if you're more confident in your own views than in others'?" Zane asked.

"You mean like most of us on the planet?" Dot chuckled.

"No, I'm making a serious point. Not all opinions are created equal. You can't run a business like a democracy. Someone has to decide."

Dot nodded. "Yes. And does that person want the benefit of other perspectives before deciding? Is he open to the possibility that the best solution may not even be on the table yet absent an honest and passionate debate? Or does he think that he surely knows better than the rest?"

"Here we go," Eliza said. "I knew there was something between the two of you."

Dot didn't say anything in response. She let her question to Zane hang in the air.

Zane shook his head. "No, Dot, I'm all in favor of different perspectives. But you still need to decide. That doesn't necessarily feel *emergent*, to use your term, but it's often what you need to do. Many times a day, actually."

"I hear you," Dot said. "One view of decisions is to choose between my view and yours—that's what Eliza was saying happens so often in Congress these days. But there's another view, and that is to see if there may not be better options than either of us has yet considered. We cut ourselves off from the possibility of that kind of choice if we keep ourselves limited to the binary *mine/your* world. Those options remain, of course, but we may discover, if we take each of our different perspectives seriously, and if we try to start with synthesis rather than avoid or delay it, that there are new and even better options to add to the mix. I've never yet been sorry for those extra options.

"Make no mistake," she continued, addressing the full group, "you can lead either way. You can stir people up and enroll them in the idea that you and they alone know the correct path, for example, as *dominators* do, and you can try to cram through your own *thesis* or *antithesis* as a result. That's an enticing and seductive message. It plays into ego, relieves people of doubt, and draws *us/them* lines that stoke energies of both fear and devotion. It can be a power-packed leadership approach. Or, as *emergents* do, you can enroll yourself on a path of inquiry and learning—on *starting with synthesis*—that keeps you open to new and better solutions even while you energetically pursue the solutions that your current understanding says are best. This openness to competing viewpoints creates its own energy, as others feel invited and welcomed into your orbit, and your openness opens them to your and others' perspectives as well. The real question is: Which of these approaches produces the more innovative, well-reasoned, and successful outcomes and solutions?

"With that said, Sam and Eliza, circling back to you, I have three questions. First, do you suppose you can oppose each other in a *dominator* way?"

They looked at each other. "Yes."

"How about in an *emergent* way?"

They each hesitated. "I suppose so. Maybe?" Sam said.

"So, this really isn't about whether you support or oppose another person, group, or their positions. Erasing a line doesn't have to mean you agree."

"Then what *does* it mean?"

"That's my third question."

13

Breaking, Blocking, Bonding, and Bridging

Let's pick a line in this room and think about it together," Dot said.

"I vote for the line between you and Zane," Eliza replied.

Dot hesitated for a moment. She looked at Zane, as if to ask, *Are you okay with that?* He shrugged.

"Okay, let's go with that one, then."

"Wonderful!" Eliza rubbed her hands together in anticipation. "So, what's going on with you two?"

"That makes it sound like you're our marriage counselor or something," Dot joked.

"Maybe more like your divorce mediator."

"Heaven help us," Zane said under his breath.

"Before we dive into details, Eliza," Dot said, "I'd like to share a story.

"About a year ago, I was conducting a workshop with a company in Huntsville, Alabama. They're a defense industry company whose relational realities were threatening them just as yours are threatening your organizations. On this occasion, I was working with the company's 20-lawyer legal team, which was led by the company's VP and General Counsel, a six-foot-six-inch-tall gentle giant of a man named Charles Enders.

"At the end of our first day together, I gave Charles an assignment. If he could pull it off, it would be the most important part of our time together. But I also told him that I wouldn't let him do it if he couldn't do it well. I asked him to think of ways he as the leader had been getting in the way of his team and how he could share those shortcomings with them. We huddled the next morning to discuss his discoveries, and I was blown away by his honesty. 'Would you be willing to share that with the team?' I asked. He told me he would—that he needed to, in fact.

"So, as we started our last session together that second afternoon, Charles came to the front of the room and said this: 'I have had the good fortune of hiring every one of you. Not many people can say they were able to assemble their own dream team. But I can, and it's incredible working with you all.

"'What you may not know, however,' he continued, 'is that I'm afraid of you. A number of you could do my job better than I can. And, honestly, I've been worried that I might lose my job to you. As a result,' he said, 'although I don't know whether you have noticed this, I have made a point of keeping the most plum and public assignments for myself, so that I can shine and be recognized.'"

Dot paused for a moment. "As an outsider watching this unfold, the looks on the faces in the room told me two things: First, they hadn't realized this; and second, they had never experienced any leader being so transparent with them.

"Charles then continued and said, 'I just want to tell you how sorry I am for that. I now see how wrong that is, and it's not how I want to be. So, today, I want to make a commitment to you. Up until now, my job has been *to keep my job*. But from now on, my job will be *to help you take my job*. That's my commitment to you.'"

Dot went silent for a moment. "That was quite an experience—to witness that kind of raw honesty in a workplace setting. It was one of the most powerful leadership moments I've ever witnessed, actually.

"But today, being with all of you, it suddenly hit me that I've been missing the biggest lesson in that whole story: *I didn't do the homework I asked Charles Enders to do!* Zane, seeing you here—and Rita and Judy, colleagues for many years—I never really considered in what ways I might have been holding *you* back. That thought hit me about an hour ago, and I haven't been able to get it out of my mind."

"You didn't hold us back at all," Rita said. "On the contrary! Everyone loved you."

"That might have been part of how I held you back," Dot responded. "Wanting to be liked can be a trap."

"I'm with Rita," Judy said. "You were an extraordinary leader for us. I'm not even sure Bellweather would exist today if not for you."

"I think I might have wanted people to believe that, Judy. But what a terrible indictment it would be of my leadership if the company couldn't survive without me."

"So how *would* you answer the question, Dot?" Zane asked. "From your perspective, do you think you held us back?"

"I think I did, Zane, yes."

He leaned in. "How?"

"Probably in a lot of ways I haven't yet considered. But one way I held *you* back, Zane, is crystal clear to me now. *I didn't help you to take my job.* You were the obvious choice to succeed me, and I should have been positioning you for that all the way along."

"But you did. You promoted me to the executive team, even over my father's wishes. I've always been grateful to you for that."

"Like I said, you were the obvious choice. I saw that immediately. But beyond putting you in a position to grow, I never really mentored you as I should have."

Zane frowned. "So, you don't think I'm ready for this."

"On one's own, no one is ready! *I* certainly wasn't. But your dad poured his soul into me. During the year before he stepped aside, he pulled me into nearly every meeting he was running. We prepared and debriefed everything. I didn't figure out why he was doing that until more than six months had passed. I just thought he wanted my input on everything. And maybe he did. But he was also pulling the curtain back on the responsibilities of his job and educating me on every nuance. But I never did any of that with you, Zane."

"Why not?" Eliza asked.

Dot paused for a moment before responding. "I think the most honest answer is because I disagreed with him. On nearly everything— strategic direction, how to work with people. Everything."

"Did you discuss all that with him?"

She grimaced. "Not really. At least, not honestly. I just disagreed and knew that we would need to do things differently from what he was wanting to do. I worked with those who were on board with what we were doing to make sure we stayed on the right path."

"So, you didn't talk with one of your most powerful colleagues because you *disagreed* with him and instead just worked around him?" Eliza said.

"I'm not proud of it, but looking back, I'd say that's mostly accurate, yes," Dot replied.

"That's not a very mature approach, if I might say."

"No, it wasn't. You're right, Eliza. Instead of working together to learn from and find a way through our differences, we each just went about our own business and tried to steer things in our preferred directions, working with our own friends and allies to do so." She looked at Eliza. "Does that sound familiar?"

Eliza stiffened against the back of her chair and momentarily closed her eyes. It was the first time Zane had ever seen her flustered, whether today or on TV. He saw her take a couple of deep breaths, which he

BREAKING, BLOCKING, BONDING, AND BRIDGING 109

recognized as centering breaths, a technique he himself used. Dot's comment had clearly knocked her off balance.

"The worst of business and politics may not be too different," Dot said. "One of the difficulties, whether in our work, personal, or political lives, is that from within our own perspectives, our actions, by definition, seem completely reasonable and justified. But I have an idea that can help to break through this.

"In the book *Bowling Alone*,[25] which chronicles the disintegration of social connections in the modern world, sociologist Robert Putnam wrote about different ways we show up when we've split ourselves from others. These ways of showing up affect what he calls *social capital*. You might think of the different levels of relation we've discussed as different levels of *social* or *relational capital*. *Division* and *subtraction* withdraw from the social capital account, driving it into the negative; *addition* is socially neutral; and *multiplication* and *compounding* invest in and increase social capital. Putnam wrote about three categories of activities that impact social capital. I've added two categories to his, and together these five categories can serve to either wake us up to how we might be driving social or relational capital into the negative or else guide us in our efforts to increase it. You might think of these as five kinds of behaviors we can engage in or attitudes we can carry that correspond with the five levels of relation.

"I'll briefly explain each of them, and then I'd like your help figuring out which category or categories have been characteristic of me in relationship with Zane. We can then apply the categories to ourselves in our various relationships and see what we discover. And, Eliza, I'll be interested in what you discover about application in the political space as well. Fair enough?"

She nodded.

"Okay, then let me introduce you to five different ways we can show up that contribute to our relational levels with others."

ACTIVITIES CORRESPONDING TO THE RELATIONAL LEVELS

2	**Compounding** Integrate		EXPANDING
1	**Multiplication** Collaborate		BRIDGING
0	**Addition** Coexist		BONDING (within like groups)
-1	**Subtraction** Resist		BLOCKING
-2	**Division** Obstruct		BREAKING

"Let's start with *breaking*. When we're breaking, we seek to gain strength from driving people apart. We divide people from each other by, among other things, driving wedges between identity groups. We play ourselves off against others—attach labels, judge, and tear down. We may belittle others or spread rumors. We view others as adversaries and attempt to gain control or power over them." She paused for a moment. "Where do we see this?"

"In our politics," Cree answered.

"On social media," Judy said.

"What level of relation do you suppose these approaches promote?"

"*Division* for sure," Jorn answered.

Dot nodded. "Let's move on to *blocking*, which corresponds to *subtraction*. When we block, we go around people, ignore them, and specifically don't consult with or involve them. We are moving our own

BREAKING, BLOCKING, BONDING, AND BRIDGING

agendas forward, and people who might oppose those agendas are our rivals. We try to outmaneuver them."

"That's what you were doing with Zane," Eliza said.

"I agree, Eliza. I was *blocking*."

"*I* was *breaking*," Zane said.

He hadn't planned to say it. The words just came out. His comment acted like a massive injection of oxygen into the room. Everyone was suddenly completely alert, but no one dared to say anything. The words echoed in the silence.

"That's what I was doing," Zane continued. "I didn't realize it at the time, but I felt you *blocking me*, and I fought against that by *breaking*. I thought that your vision for the company wasn't big enough, and I did what I felt I had to do to secure a much larger future for us. I'd probably do it again if we had it to do over."

Dot looked at him for a moment. "And I was trying to stop you without actually working with you on it. In the end, I think that's part of the reason things ended up the way they did. If I had it to do over again, I'd do it very differently."

"How?"

"Well, let's explore a few more of these categories, and then we can consider that question together.

"The next category after breaking is *bonding*. Bonding refers to how we tend to huddle with people on our own side of lines. We support each other, we mourn with each other, and we strengthen each other. This can be really positive, as we can find community there. And for groups that have been historically discriminated against, bonding like this provides an essential lifeline. But it does invite people to look inward and stay in homogenous groups, which makes it more difficult to benefit from different perspectives and life experiences.

"In organizations, bonding is associated with siloing and corresponds to the *addition* level of relation. Of course, there's nothing negative about bonding with one's team or department, but if that comes at the expense of reaching out to and including others, the bonding comes at a real cost. It creates echo chambers and maintains lines.

"Which brings me to *bridging*. Bridging refers to efforts to step out beyond one's group—to reach across lines, seek out differences, and be curious about other viewpoints. When bridging, we accept and even embrace the benefits of bonding, but from these benefits we recognize the greater benefit of bridging to and connecting with other groups beyond our own. From a group perspective, *bridging* is one group reaching out to another in the form of a person who is willing to cross over lines. Organizationally, it corresponds to the *multiplication* level of relation, where we see significant levels of cooperation. However, and this is important, bridging alone still assumes the existence of lines that need to be crossed over. A world of no lines—or of expanded lines, if you will—is the world of *expanding*.

"Before we get to *expanding*, however, let's apply what we've just been talking about. Zane, you asked me what I would have done differently in our work together. I already said that I was engaging in *blocking*, and you said that you were *breaking*. I suppose both of us put energy into *bonding* as well, with our own allies. But how about *bridging*? I didn't bridge toward you. I kept to myself and to my own. How about you?"

"Same."

"Do you think there might have been advantages had we bridged?"

Zane thought about it. Truth was, he was comfortable with where he was, and with where the company was. "I'm not sure. I don't know if you would have ever agreed with me."

"I might not have. But that's not why we bridge—to get others to agree with us. That's a *dominator* stance. We bridge to see the world from a different place. Bridging is traveling—not physically, but psychologically. It's a way of seeing new places, meeting people anew, encountering different perspectives, and in the process learning to appreciate and care about them. That's what I would have done if I had it to do over again, Zane. I would have *bridged*. I really would have wanted to expand—to

BREAKING, BLOCKING, BONDING, AND BRIDGING 113

make water. But you can't get there without first being willing to bridge. I regret that I didn't make any efforts to do that. I'm profoundly sorry about that."

Zane waved it off. "Don't worry about it. Everything worked out as it should have."

"Did it, though?"

Zane didn't reply.

"Maybe we can pick that back up tomorrow," Dot said.

Zane glanced at his watch. He was surprised to discover that it was already 5 PM. And he was even more surprised to realize that he hadn't checked the time all day.

"Can I say something here?" Eliza asked.

"Since when did you start asking for permission?" Dexter joked.

Eliza laughed. "A few minutes ago, someone mentioned social media—Judy, I think it might have been you. I'm personally very troubled by what social media is doing to our children and, by extension, to our communities. In fact, I've co-written a bill that's in committee right now seeking to regulate social media in more effective ways. It occurs to me that every social media outlet I can think of specializes in the divisive forms of social interaction you've just shared—*breaking, blocking*, and *bonding*. We throw insults at each other, mischaracterize each other, and gather into subcultures that share the same views, entrenching us even further into our own ways of thinking. I'm wondering what a social media platform might look like that was built on *bridging* and *expanding*. Or whether it would be possible to create such a platform."

"That's an interesting question," Arlo said. "I'm thinking about the same kind of question closer to home. What would legislative work on Capitol Hill look like if we focused on *bridging*—and *expanding*, too, I suppose, although we haven't really explored that yet—rather than on the *breaking, blocking*, and same-party *bonding* that currently characterizes our politics? What would that kind of politics look like? I'm reminded of a part of our political history that might give us some clues."

"Yeah? What in particular?" Eliza asked.

"I'm thinking about the Constitutional Convention in Philadelphia in the summer of 1787. For the benefit of any here who aren't familiar with the story, 55 delegates gathered to revise the failing Articles of Confederation that had held the 13 states loosely together since the Revolutionary War. It soon became clear, however, that they needed to completely overhaul the country's governmental structure to preserve the nation.

"As the weeks went on, however, their efforts ground toward an impasse, which would have ended the American experiment almost before it began. The main battle was over states' rights. The large states supported James Madison's Virginia Plan, which called for two legislative bodies, the membership of which would depend on the population of each state. The small states didn't like that, of course, and supported William Paterson's New Jersey Plan, which reduced the legislative bodies from two to one and called for that single legislative body to be composed of single representatives from each state, each with equal voting power.

"But two things happened that changed the course of our nation. First, after arguing with each other every day, the delegates gathered in social settings every evening—eating together, drinking, telling stories, and building relationships. They met in taverns, citizens' homes, and, on occasion, in the home of Benjamin Franklin, who shared stories from his extraordinary life and created an atmosphere where they could do the same with each other.

"The second thing that happened was that one of them, Roger Sherman of Connecticut, submitted a possible compromise to their political impasse. He proposed a legislative branch of two chambers—one reflecting representation by population, which the large states favored, and the other composed of two representatives from each state regardless of state size, each with a single vote. Legislation had to pass both bodies—what we now know as the House and the Senate—to become law, so the interests of both the large and small states would be advanced and protected.

"They continued to debate the details, but this new idea opened a space for them to make progress together. It was a solution that likely wouldn't have been found had the sides not argued vigorously for their positions and had they not, individually and as a group, developed what George Washington called a 'spirit of amity' and 'mutual deference' toward one another.[26]

"We wouldn't have a country today if the delegates hadn't *bridged*. And they instituted structural rules to make that more likely—daily attendance was mandatory, for example, no talking or reading was allowed when someone was speaking, they did not keep an official record on votes or the proceedings so that people could vigorously debate according to belief and conscience, and so on."

"Hmm, that's really interesting, Arlo, thank you," Eliza said. "I wasn't aware of all that. We certainly don't spend much time anymore outside of our official hours with members of the opposite party. And we'd have to institute many new systems and processes to replace those that today incentivize breaking and blocking. But the fact that we can still disagree, as our political forebearers vigorously did, while bridging and expanding, at least makes it theoretically possible to do politics that way."

"Well, that's a start!" Dot said. "How about business? Do you all see how a *bridging* approach to business would be more promising than a *breaking*, *blocking*, and one-side-only *bonding* approach?"

"I do for sure," Rita said.

"Me too," Jorn agreed. Others around the room nodded.

"Then we'll need to take this to the next level—to *expanding*. To do that, I'll need to introduce you to the fascinating but misunderstood work of Martin Buber. However, given the time, we'll have to dive into those insights first thing tomorrow.

"Before we break for the day, however, let's review what we've learned."

14

Putting It Together

"To begin with," Dot said, "what did we learn from Ricardo's tic-tac-toe match with Eliza?"

"To go first!" Eliza said.

Dot cracked up. "Yes, to go first, that's right! And what else did we learn, *no matter who* goes first?"

"That every move is in anticipation or response to something else," Pam answered. "No one thing stands on its own."

"Do you remember the First Law of Relation that Ricardo attached to that insight?" Dot asked.

"Yes, I think so," Pam replied. "Since we ourselves are the ones seeing everything we're observing, every observation is an intersection of ourselves and the world. Which means that we never see separate things. *All we ever see is relation.*"

"Yes, Pam, excellent! That's the First Law. Do any of you remember the other laws of relation?"

"With the painting as an analogy," Sam said, "we learned that everything is made of relation, all the way down."

"Yes," Dot agreed, "that is the Second Law of Relation: *Everything is built by relation*. Which is true of us too. So, *how* are we built through relation? What, in our lives, functions like the *dots*, so to speak," she said with a smile, "of Seurat's painting?"

"Our *interactions*," Jorn answered. "That was the point Ricardo illustrated with the experiment about light. What light is depends on how we interact with it, just as who we are depends on how we interact with others. The two relationships we each thought about illustrated this as well, as we show up as very different people in each of them. Our interactions are the dots that paint our lives."

"Yes, Jorn, which explains the Third Law of Relation: *How we interact is who we are*.

"So, who remembers the Fourth Law?" Dot asked.

"That was the *making water* point, right?" Rita answered. "Differences coming together are what make the new possible."

"Yes, Rita. And Ricardo captured that idea in the Fourth Law of Relation: *We progress by uniting*. Excellent.

"Next, who remembers the five levels of relation we discussed?"

Arlo raised his hand. "*Division, subtraction, addition, multiplication*, and *compounding*."

"Great, thank you, Arlo. And why should we care about those levels in organizations?"

"Because performance increases with each level."

"Why not just work on individuals to improve performance? And on teams? Can't you do that?"

Pam raised her hand. "Yes, you can. In fact, that's what most everyone does. But you and Ricardo have been showing us how the science points in a different direction. Since individuals and teams are not separate things but manifestations of relation, it makes sense to tackle the relational nodes themselves. And as is evidently the case with quantum computing, a relational approach with human beings may similarly enable much higher levels of energy and possibility."

"Are you convinced of that?"

PUTTING IT TOGETHER

"I'm not sure. It makes sense, but it's such a different way of thinking about things that it's still settling in."

"Fair enough.

"And what about the relational maps we constructed—both the interpersonal one in this room, and the sample map we built around the relations of different organizational departments? What is the utility of such maps?"

"They make the invisible visible," Judy said. "They are ways of filling in the space in a company's org chart—to see what's really going on in the space between us, which is where everything happens."

"Can you see how you can utilize such maps to track and drive real change in organizations?"

"For sure. I've been thinking about building one with my operations team at Bellweather. Actually, two—one that charts the levels of relation within ops, and a second that tracks them between ops and all the other parts of the company. I'm pretty energized by the possibility of that kind of visibility."

Zane found himself nodding. That kind of mapping seemed like a good idea.

"And who can explain the relationship between the levels of relation and the different quadrants we discussed? Let's take this in two steps. First, what are the four quadrants, and then, how are they related to the levels of relation?"

"I think I can explain it," Zane said. "First of all, the four quadrants are *behavior*, *attitude*, *structure*, and *community*. They become visible as quadrants when you apply the two distinctions you made to organizations: first, that an organization is a collective whole that is comprised of individual people, and second, that both the individuals and the collective have outsides and insides. So, the outside and the inside of an individual are her *behaviors* and *attitudes*, respectively, and the outside and inside of the group are its *structures* on the one hand and its *community* on the other." He paused, a faint smile showing on his face. "Did I get that right?"

Dot smiled. "Not bad. Now, can you explain what those quadrants have to do with the levels of relation?"

"Well, I think you said that the way we create the conditions for relationships to improve is by making the elements of each of those quadrants more conducive for higher levels of relation—improving *behaviors*, *attitudes*, *structures*, and *community*. Or something like that."

"Yes, very good, Zane. And does that seem right to you—as a strategic approach, I mean?"

He thought about it for a moment. "It doesn't seem obviously wrong, I'll say that. I think the quadrants do cover the territory of most of the things you would want to work on. As you know, at Bellweather, we put a lot of emphasis on what you're calling *attitude*. We're organizing our efforts around what we call *Seeing Human*, which I think is congruent with what we've been talking about."

"Perhaps," she replied. "Or perhaps not."

Zane's eyebrows rose in surprise. "Hmm. I guess I'd like to hear more about that."

"We'll get to it tomorrow," she replied.

Then, to the group, she said, "Just a couple more questions before we close it down for the day. The first of those is this: If you are trying to build a unified team, does that mean you want to get everyone to think and do the same?"

"No," Jorn said. "I don't think so."

"Why not, Jorn?"

"That goes to the point you and Ricardo were making about the importance of difference—like oxygen and hydrogen holding on to each other to make water. In an odd way, unity seems to require difference."

"Exactly right, Jorn. Unity is routinely misunderstood. It is a state of differences being in relation in a unified way, not a state of sameness. What might that have to do with the difference between *dominator* versus *emergent* approaches to leadership?"

"*Dominators* don't have an appreciation or respect for difference," Jorn answered, "whereas *emergent* leaders do. Dominators push their

PUTTING IT TOGETHER 121

theses and *antitheses*, but emergent leaders value *synthesis*. In fact, I think you said that they turn the normal pattern around and even *start* with synthesis."

"Yes, and how do they do that?"

"By seeking out and considering opposing perspectives."

"Very good, Jorn, thank you. That's excellent. So, two more questions for the rest of you. First, how are the activities of *breaking, blocking, bonding, bridging,* and *expanding* related to the levels of relation?"

"Aren't they just different titles for them?" Sam asked.

"You're on the right track, Sam. You are right that the two are correlated. However, I would say that *breaking, blocking, bonding, bridging,* and *expanding* are looking at each of those levels through the lens of how the parties themselves are acting, while the levels of relation are focusing on the state of the relationships themselves. Does that make sense?"

Sam nodded. "So, you're saying that we contribute to the level of relation we might be experiencing by what we ourselves are bringing or not bringing to it in the *behavior* and *attitude* quadrants, and that *breaking,* and so on, are ways to categorize our own contributions."

"I like that, yes," Dot replied. "That's a really good way to say it."

"Anything else from today that anyone would like to mention?" she then asked the group.

"I was struck by the work of that paleontologist Ricardo mentioned," Pam said. "You know, the guy who showed how growth and progress always come through the process of different things *compressing* against each other, then *converging,* and then yielding the *emergence* of something new—like hydrogen, oxygen, and water."

"Yes, Pam," Ricardo said. "And that scientist's name was Pierre Teilhard de Chardin. I recommend his work to you if you're up for some interesting reading."

"For sure."

"I'll point you to a couple of books when we break."[27]

"I think I heard Ricardo say *break!*" Dot continued. "Well done today, everyone! We'll start tomorrow at precisely 9 AM. Right here. If you would like to fly rather than battle the DC traffic, talk to Zane about his helicopter! See you again in the morning."

After wishing everyone a good evening, Zane walked out of the room. Deep in thought, he ascended the stairs to exit the building. Before leaving, he turned to look again at the words Dot had pointed out when they entered that morning.

Substance so stirred at its depth
To result in a change in essence
Opening a path for transformation
From solitariness
To synthesis

A few things now stood out to him. *From solitariness to synthesis* clearly sounded like a move toward relation. And he wondered if the word *synthesis* might be a reference to *Hegel's Spiral* or to Teilhard de Chardin's ideas about *convergence* and *emergence*. But *substance so stirred at its depth*, and a *change in essence*? He didn't know what either of those might be referring to. Still wondering about it, he turned to exit the building.

As he walked toward the helicopter, he took his phone out of his pocket, opened his contacts, and scrolled to *Jackson*. After hesitating for a moment, he pressed on his name.

The phone started ringing.

PART III

EXPANDING

15

Ruminations

At 8:10 AM the next morning, Zane was stuck in early northbound traffic on the George Washington Memorial Parkway in Virginia. No helicopter today. That had been for pageantry and show in front of the company the day before. Today, he, Judy, Cree, and Rita were on their own. *Ironic, given the prior day's theme of relation*, he thought.

He relived his phone conversation with Jackson from the evening before. It had been short and somewhat awkward, but at least they had talked. What do you say to a son you've barely spoken to in six months? How can you pick such a relationship back up like nothing had happened? *Maybe I should have apologized for going quiet over these months*, he thought. Instead, they talked about school and golf, which had been their pattern for years. Just guy talk—nothing deep, pretty surface, engaged but at a thin level. *But at least we're talking again.*

Still, Zane felt a bit empty. He wanted more. Of what, however, he wasn't entirely sure.

He had thought about calling Laney as well but couldn't bring himself to do it. *Maybe write her a note?* He couldn't do that either. *If I can't mean it, there's no point in doing it,* he reasoned.

Almost lost amidst his thoughts about his soon-to-be ex-wife and son was his daughter, Allison. She was a year younger than Jackson and attending Cornell. Zane hadn't really been in much contact with her of late, either, but he didn't feel any resistance in himself about her the way he felt with Jackson, and their conversations, when they had them, felt freer and easier.

His mind turned to the levels of relation they had discussed the day before. His relationship with Jackson was definitely at the *subtraction* level, the resistance he felt being the obvious indicator of that. *Toward Laney? Division for sure. What about with Allison?* He didn't feel any resentment or resistance toward her. But the fact remained that they rarely spoke. *I suppose the best rating I could put on it would be addition,* he thought. *Multiplication and compounding?* He couldn't see any.

Division, subtraction, addition—my relationships with the people closest to me. He felt the hint of tears coming. *What the hell is happening? Why have we become so estranged?*

He thought about the four quadrants Dot had introduced— *behavior, attitude, structure,* and *community.* He could see how his own attitudes and behaviors were contributing to the divisions between them. As a rule, he wasn't very communicative, despite his studies and training. Music moved him, as did ideas. But people? Not so much. *Why is that?* he wondered. *And is it a problem?*

What about family structures and processes, and family community? Culturally, they certainly had an ethos of hard work and achievement. Zane's father had drilled that into him, and he had done the same with his own children. This was a point on which he and Laney had agreed. In fact, they sometimes talked about how they had done a pretty good job raising their children together. They just hadn't been good for each other, and the absence of tenderness and love between them had contributed to a rather austere atmosphere in the home. Whether for

RUMINATIONS

that or other reasons, their children had always preferred gathering with their friends elsewhere, which left Zane and Laney home alone together, with no diversions to hide the stiff awkwardness and hurt between them.

In the structural area, they had been moderately churchgoing as a family, and Laney's family was big on family gatherings, which meant that they had traveled to Kentucky many more times than Zane had wanted. So, there was at least a container of traditions and practices they had engaged in together. With the kids now gone, however, all of that had mostly evaporated. Laney went to her family gatherings alone and Zane's religion was mostly work, golf, and writing his music. Although his music writing sessions had lately shrunk almost to zero.

His mind turned to Dot's distinction between *dominator* and *emergent* leadership approaches. His father had been a dominator, and Zane had rebelled against it. In his later years, however, Frank Savage's stance had changed. His treatment of Dot was indicative of this change, as he had learned to listen to, trust, and rely upon her, ultimately elevating her to replace him. His changes toward Zane had been more subtle.

Until Zane was 14, his bedroom was beneath the stairs to the basement, a space only slightly larger than Harry Potter's closet. The stairs down to his little room were unfinished, which caused his father's footfalls to echo through the walls whenever he descended them to "visit" after disciplining Zane.

A particular scene in this room, after being disciplined by his father, came to his memory. He remembered the upstairs door opening and his father descending the wooden steps. He knocked softly on the door with a single knuckle and asked, "Is it okay if I come in?" Despite Zane's anger just moments before, he heard himself say, "Yes." His father then came in and sat next to him on the bed. He didn't say what Zane had done was okay, and he didn't apologize for punishing him. On the contrary, he talked about how much he expected of him. *Ever the disciplinarian,* Zane thought. *Performance, performance, performance.*

But as Zane thought about it now, he realized something he'd never thought of before: His father *always* came down to talk to him after disciplining him. He always knocked with that one-knuckle knock. He always asked if it was okay if he came in. He always sat next to him on that bed.

As Zane saw his father through the lens of the very project of fatherhood that Zane himself was currently failing, he felt the tears returning. *He always loved me. Even back then.*

By now, Zane had crossed the Potomac River into Maryland and was approaching the intersection of Macarthur Boulevard and Falls Road. A left turn would take him down to Great Falls. With Glenstone as his destination, he bent to the right. He was about 15 minutes away. The dense forest around him began yielding to the beautiful estates situated amid the gentle slopes of this part of Potomac, Maryland. *Pull yourself together, Zane.*

He began thinking about the people in the room—his own colleagues, Judy, Cree, and Rita; the people from Congress, Eliza, Sam, Dexter, and Arlo; and the team from PERC, Jorn, Pam . . . He stumbled on the other two names. *Who were they again?* And, of course, he fixated on Dot and Ricardo.

Although he couldn't explain why, his feelings toward Dot had moderated. Perhaps it was the open but still respectful way she had discussed their differences. Or maybe it was just the fact that he was with her in person again and not just in his head about her. Ricardo, however, was a different story. If anything, he was more skeptical of him than ever, although he wasn't sure why.

A few minutes later, he pulled into the Glenstone parking lot next to the black SUVs he'd seen from the helicopter the day before. The other groups, it seemed, had come together again.

Upon entering the door of the main building, Zane glanced once more at the words above him on the wall.

Substance so stirred at its depth
To result in a change in essence
Opening a path for transformation
From solitariness
To synthesis

After the thoughts he'd had on his drive, he recognized himself in the first line.

I suppose I have been stirred, he thought. *But in my depths?* He thought about it. *I don't know. Do I want that?*

He paused before turning to descend the stairs and looked at the verse again. *What would a change in my essence mean? And would I even want it?* Unsure, he turned for the stairs.

As he descended them, Laney's words came to him again . . .

You don't care about anything or anyone but yourself.

16

Trapped in Our Heads

"Welcome back, everyone," Dot said. "I hope you all had a restful evening."

"A fine thing to say after waking us up so much that we couldn't sleep!" Dexter said.

"What was on your mind, old friend?"

"*Old friend?*" Eliza asked

"A *very* old friend, yes. Dex and I went to high school together in Cincinnati. And, as it happens, he's the reason I'm here."

"Okay," Eliza said slowly. "You got some 'splainin' to do."

Dot laughed. "I'm afraid it's not the story you're hoping for! After leaving Bellweather, I took a little time off to figure out what to do next. Then one day, out of the blue, Dex called. We'd followed each other's careers over the years and occasionally crossed paths at official events, but until then neither of us had ever reached out to the other. He told me about a task force he was working with that needed the right kind of corporate leadership. Before I knew it, I was in DC interviewing with members of the president's staff. And that's ultimately how I ended up here, almost two years ago."

"*Here* meaning the task force?" Cree jumped in.

"Yes."

"And can I ask who else is on it?"

"Somehow I knew you'd be the person to ask that, Cree!" Dot laughed again. "Ricardo is part of the team, along with about 50 other leaders selected from the business, governmental, political, educational, scientific, media, religious, and financial sectors. It's a broad coalition tasked with tackling issues related to disintegration within our institutions and across the social landscape."

"And Dexter, here, is part of it too?"

"I'll let you answer that, Dex."

"I'm not on the task force, no," he said. "It's an executive branch effort, not a legislative one. But the president did consult with me about it and asked if I had people I would recommend."

"So, the team is all Democrats?" Cree followed up.

"I don't think you have reason to know my politics, Cree," Dot replied. "But it would be exceedingly ironic if a team tasked with overcoming divides were built only from one side of the political aisle."

"With all due respect, that didn't answer my question."

Whoa now, Cree, don't go crazy here, Zane thought.

Dot smiled. "I don't know the exact mix of political affiliations, but we've been careful to make sure we have people spread across all the spectrums, political and otherwise. I believe Eliza and Arlo were consulted for recommendations the same way Dex was. Am I right?"

They both nodded.

"And are you satisfied with the mix of views of the people on the task force?"

"Yes," Arlo answered. "I like the group you've assembled."

"I'm supportive," Eliza said.

TRAPPED IN OUR HEADS

"That's not the strongest recommendation I've ever heard," Cree commented.

"Well, the proof, as they say, is in the puddin'," Eliza responded. "I like the mix of people and perspectives, but I want to see what they actually do. That's a large part of why I'm here."

"Wait, so you all *chose* to be here?" Zane asked.

"More or less," Eliza answered.

"Not us," Jorn said. "We were, shall I say, 'strongly encouraged not to miss it'—by Arlo here, in fact. Or was it rather Senator Morris on the Energy Committee?"

"Both of us," Arlo answered. "And I'm glad you got the message."

Dot paused for more questions. "Anything else, Cree?"

He shook his head.

"Okay, then. I want to start our day by talking about this room. We chose it for two reasons. First, I think you'll agree it's a stunning space. We're in the building, but it feels like we're joined with the outside."

Everyone nodded and began commenting about how amazing it was.

"Except," Dot continued, "and this is the second reason we chose this room, we *aren't* joined with what's outside. We're separated in a way that masks our separation. From within this room, we can see what's outside, but we aren't joined with it, even though the visual field makes it seem like we are. It's a satisfyingly comfortable place to be. But it's also false, a trick, an illusion."

She paused for a moment before continuing. "Does anyone here like getting out in nature?"

Cree raised his hand. Zane did not see that coming.

"It's my favorite place to be—away from people," he said.

Well, that makes sense, Zane thought.

"Communing with the trees."

Oh brother.

"And does it feel the same way encountering nature from within this room, Cree?"

He shook his head. "Not at all. I don't *feel* the trees from here. I can see them and can perhaps even appreciate them, but I'm not in conversation with them. The experience from here is, well, two-dimensional and shallow. Out there, it's much deeper."

"Hmm, I can feel how much you love being in nature, Cree. Thank you."

He acknowledged Dot's comment with a nod.

"This room is a metaphor for how we live our lives much of the time," Dot continued. "We see what's 'outside' us and feel like we're connected with it. But we aren't—we *aren't* joined with what is out there. Instead, we're stuck in our own room, gazing from behind our own glass. Breaking free from this illusion and separation is what the work of Martin Buber helps us to do."

The mention of Buber excited Zane, and he had to admit he had Dot to thank for that. She had trained him and most of the rest of Bellweather on his work years ago, and Bellweather's leadership training program drew heavily from those insights.

"To frame up Buber's work, I want to show you a depiction of the divide that has split the world since the time of René Descartes.

THE MODERN MIND/WORLD SPLIT

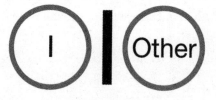

"I think therefore I am." (René Descartes)

Assumption: The separate mind/self is fundamental.

"You'll remember Ricardo discussing how Descartes's hugely influential work split the modern world into billions of disconnected pieces. The starting point of his philosophical project—'I think therefore I am'—puts each of us, and specifically our thinking minds, on one side of a line from everyone and everything else. Descartes drew us into this room—cut off, separated, yet able to peer out from behind our divides to observe, speculate, and see. This is what creates the illusion of connection—after all, we can *see* each other! Ergo, it seems we're together! But, alas, no. A life characterized by observing and seeing others is a life of separation from them."

Wait, that's not right, Zane thought to himself. *Doesn't it depend on how you're seeing others? Isn't that what you talked about for years—using Buber to do it?*

"If Descartes *divides* us from each other," Dot continued, "Buber puts us back together again. And the way he does it is genius. It's the key to understanding what *expanding* is, as well as being the portal to the highest level of relation—*compounding*."

Dot displayed the following diagram . . .

BUBER'S HYPHEN

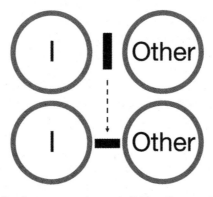

The line between us does not divide—it connects us.
We are connected, as it were, by a hyphen.

"Buber's first move was to turn Descartes's line 90 degrees and make it into a hyphen. What do you suppose that move means?"

"It looks like it means that there's no me without others," Pam answered, "no *separate me* but only *connected me*—like Ricardo was sharing yesterday. Whereas Descartes's approach seems to imply that I am me independent of others."

"Yes, Pam, that's a great way of encapsulating what Ricardo helped us to understand yesterday. Human beings are fundamentally of one another. Our bodies are formed from our genetic histories. We think, speak, and ideate in words we've acquired from others. Our emotional experience depends on our experience of others. And we develop as human beings through our interactions with others—both influencing and being influenced. In fact, even the choices we make are, to some significant degree, influenced by the people around us—by peer pressure we might feel, for example, and by the behaviors that are deemed acceptable by the groups of which we're a part. We choose, yes, but we choose within this relational context, which is already influencing *how* we choose.

"Let me give you a quick and interesting example of this. A friend of mine ran an experiment on himself. For two separate years, he resolved to watch news from only a single channel per year. For Year 1, he chose a channel with a political bent very different from his own. He wanted to see if limiting inputs to that sole and different viewpoint would affect his own worldviews.

"His supposition was that it wouldn't make any difference. He's a smart, logical, careful thinker, and he was sure he could cut through any crap. He was confident that his views couldn't be manipulated or changed.

"However, by the end of that year, his political views had completely transformed. By then he saw the world the way the news channel he watched that year had painted the world to be. He was surprised by that result, but happy that he was seeing things more correctly than before.

TRAPPED IN OUR HEADS

"But then he ran the experiment again. For the second year, he switched to a different sole source for his news—a channel with views diametrically opposed to the ones espoused by the channel he had been watching in Year 1. Even more than before, he was convinced that his opinions couldn't be swayed by a different viewpoint. He changed the channel fully expecting that he would end that year with the same views he then held.

"However, after a year watching and listening to the news and broadcasts of this different station, his views had been completely transformed once again. He had disavowed most of the views he held at the end of the year prior."

"That's crazy," Judy said.

"Yes, it is," Dot agreed. "Forgetting for a moment the uncommon discipline it takes to stick to such a plan, what do my friend's experiments suggest?"

"That our views are malleable," Judy replied.

"Yes. And when you think about it in terms of relationality, it suggests that we don't hold our own opinions but the opinions of those we are listening to.

"So, for all these reasons and more," Dot continued, "Buber says that the separations we perceive are an illusion. That doesn't mean there is no *I* or *self*, but it does mean that there is no *I-in-itself* but only *I-in-relation*. Rather than being separated by walls, we are joined together by hyphens, our mutual influences mingling both between and within us.

"However, Buber described two very different ways to be in relation across the hyphen. He called the first approach an *I-It* orientation and, depending on which translation of his work you are reading, the second is an *I-Thou* or *I-You* orientation.[28] For our purposes, we'll use the *I-You* rendition. Our impact on others and their impact on us depend fundamentally on which way we engage—two ways that are almost universally misunderstood."

Dot showed the following on the screen . . .

TWO WAYS OF BEING WITH OTHERS

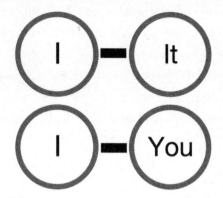

"What do you think each of these means? And how do you think they might differ from each other?"

"This is what you emphasized with us at Bellweather," Zane answered. "We can see others either as objects or as people—as *Its* or as *Yous*."

"That *is* what I used to think, Zane. You're right. But like most people who study Buber only superficially, I misunderstood him. As a result, I misrepresented his work to you and everyone else at Bellweather, and I am truly sorry for that."

Zane looked at her, stunned. "How so?"

"I want you to imagine something, Zane."

"Okay."

"Imagine that instead of a beautiful landscape outside this window, there were people out there. Could you see them as people who *matter like you matter*, as we used to say at Bellweather?"

He thought about it. "Sure."

"And yet, you'd still be locked in on this side of the glass, even while you're seeing them that way."

"Well, I don't know about being locked in," he replied. "I could always go out there and join them."

"Of course. But you could see them as people even if you didn't, isn't that right?"

"I suppose so, yes."

"Which is why what Buber is saying is very different from what I previously thought. Anything that can be done without actually encountering each other allows us to maintain a separated way of living. You can't get out of this room merely by trying to see differently from within it. Buber was talking about an entirely different kind of change than merely a change to how one is seeing."

"Then I guess I don't understand what he's saying."

"I was in the same place as you, Zane. Until I read something by the biographer and scholar who knew Buber's work the best. He said this: 'It must be understood first that [*You*] is not an object but a *relationship*. If this is not understood, [Buber] will not be understood.'"[29]

Dot paused. "Let me repeat that: *You*, the way Buber is using the term, is neither an object nor a person but a *relationship*. He was not making a distinction between *seeing others as objects* on the one hand or *as people* on the other. Rather, he was making a distinction between merely *seeing* others—whether as objects *or* as people—and entering into relationship with them."

"Huh?" Zane was confused.

"That was my reaction too," Dot said. "Until I slowly began to understand: The resolution to Buber's puzzle, and the doorway to *expanding* and *compounding*, is located not in the words *It* or *You*, but in the hyphen itself."

17

Buber's Hyphen

A couple of questions for you, Zane," Dot continued. "First, let's think about the view from this room again. Where are you located when you're looking out at the landscape?"

"Me? I guess I'm located in this room."

"Yes. Which means that you're not actually *with* the landscape. You're separated from it."

"I suppose so, yes. Although you can hardly tell that from here."

"Agreed. Which is why the illusion is so enticing. You could spend all your time in this room and believe you were connected with what's outside, even though you aren't. In that respect, this room is a metaphor for the *I-It* way of being. We can observe things or people from in here, experience ourselves looking at them, and even decide how we want to see them. But we aren't actually with them except in our heads, where things are tidily organized in ways that make sense to or comfort us.

"In a particular passage that completely rocked me, as I realized it meant I previously had misunderstood his work, Buber put it this way: 'I perceive something. I am sensible of something. I imagine something. I

142   YOU AND WE

will something. I feel something. I think something . . . This and the like together establish the realm of *It*.'[30] Buber called this 'psychologizing the world'—our tendency to take the world into our minds and believe that we are interacting with the world when we're actually interacting with our own experience or representation of it."

"Isn't that inescapable?" Zane asked. "Since we ourselves are doing the seeing, as Ricardo talked about yesterday, won't it always be the case that we're interacting with our own representations?"

"Not necessarily," Dot replied.

"Okay," Zane said slowly, trying to see where she was going.

"In order to get at that difference," she said, "let me ask you another question: When you're trying to see others as people, where is that activity located?"

"I'm not sure what you mean. It's not really located anywhere. It's more psychological than physical."

"So, it's located in your head, then," Dot said.

"Well, okay. Yes."

"And where is the *concept* of a person—the thing you are trying to see the other as—located?"

"In my mind, I suppose?"

"Exactly. Now, hold onto that insight for a moment. I want to come back to Cree about something.

"So, Cree, you said that it's different being out among the trees and landscape than it is observing or admiring them from within this room—is that right?"

"Entirely."

"You said something to the effect that there's no depth in the experience of just looking at the trees from here as compared to being in and amongst them—is that right?"

"Yes. Out there, I feel moved in a deep kind of way. From here, however, the most I could say is that I enjoy and appreciate looking at them. And those aren't the same things. Observing is unidirectional. It's a way of keeping spiritual and emotional distance. But when you're out there, although it may sound weird, it's like you're in conversation."

Who are you? Zane thought to himself.

"As a person whose idea of camping is staying at a nice hotel," Dot said, "I obviously don't know nature like you do, Cree. I have so much to learn from you!"

He shrugged. "There's nothing keeping you from it. Except yourself."

"Touché!" Dot laughed.

"I don't mean anything by it. I think I might listen to trees better than I listen to people, to be honest. So, I think I have a lot to learn from you about the latter. After all, we're all here in this room together. And in our organizations together. And communities. There's nothing separating us except ourselves. Can't blame the damn window for that."

Zane thought he knew Cree, but as his comments accumulated, he realized he didn't. He looked over at him. *You are an interesting man.*

"If we put Zane's and Cree's insights together," Dot said, "we can unlock what Buber is saying. *Within*—that is, in one's head—is *I-It*. *Between*, in the hyphen, is *I-You*."

She displayed the following . . .

THE CORE DIFFERENCE BETWEEN THE TWO WAYS

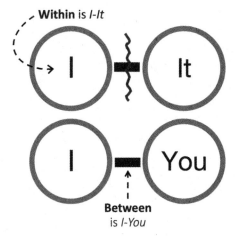

"Again, the key thing to understand is that the difference between *I-It* and *I-You* is not in the words that follow the hyphen but rather depends on where the action is happening. For Descartes, who assumed we're fundamentally divided from others, the action is always necessarily in the *I*—in things that the *I has* or *possesses*. In what *I'm* thinking, for example, what *I'm* feeling, what or how *I'm* seeing, and so on. But Buber is saying that since we're actually fundamentally connected, the action doesn't have to be in the *I*. There's another possibility—that it can be in the relationship or hyphen itself, or in what Buber calls *the between*. There is more to our lives than simply the psychological workings of our brains. If the action is in my head, that's *I-It*—separate, detached, clinical, third person. In that case, I'm still living within Descartes's paradigm, with an effectual wall or pane of glass between myself and others. If I'm engaging with another in a genuine second-person encounter, on the other hand, that's *I-You*. 'Whoever says *You* . . .' Buber writes, '*has* nothing. But he stands in relation.'"[31]

Zane studied the diagram. He was struggling to ground his entire experience at Bellweather around Buber's work with what Dot was now saying. "So where is *seeing people as people*?" he asked.

"Well, is seeing others *within* or *between*?"

"Within," he answered begrudgingly.

"And if it's *within*, is that *I-You* or *I-It*?"

He didn't answer.

"*I-You* happens *between*, not *within*," Dot repeated. "The English-speaking world routinely misunderstands this, partly because of something that's lost in translation from the original German to English. And it just so happens that Ricardo is a native German speaker. He can help us understand what we're missing in English."

"Wait, you're German?" Eliza asked. "What kind of a German name is Ricardo Bloom?"

He laughed. "My mom is actually Spanish."

"That explains *Ricardo*, but *Bloom*?"

"When my father's family came to this country, they changed the spelling of their last name—from B-l-u-m to B-l-o-o-m. Spelled with

BUBER'S HYPHEN

145

a *u*, Blum is a perfectly German name, I can assure you." He waited a moment. "Are you worried about my middle name too?"

"Oh, stop it. Move along."

He smiled. "Okay, then. How are you all enjoying this exploration of Martin Buber's work?"

"It's pretty interesting, actually," Jorn said.

Tim Costello, PERC's VP of Governmental Affairs, raised his hand.

"Yes, Tim," Ricardo said, inviting him to share. "And welcome to the conversation."

"I've been taking everything in, believe me. I just process things privately."

"Before coming here this morning," he continued, "my wife and I got into an argument."

"Oh, do tell!" Eliza said.

"No, I don't think so." He smiled shyly. "But long story short, I keep replaying the argument in my head and keep feeling frustrated and angry about it. I'm just busy with thoughts in my head. It's all *within*, not *between*. The argument is over, and my wife isn't even here!"

"Well, given that your wife isn't here," Zane said, "the only way you *could* be with her at the moment is in your head."

Ricardo nodded. "Zane raises an important point. We need to be careful not to think that being in one's head—being *I-It*—is bad, while being *I-You* is good. That's not what Buber was saying at all. We have heads for a reason, and feelings, thoughts, and concepts aren't bad. Which, I might add, is a relief for a university professor! Furthermore, memories of experiences with others, while necessarily in one's head and therefore *I-It*, are an essential part of life and can be very positive. However, being in one's head, *especially while interacting with others*, is different from truly meeting others outside one's head. The German-language point Dot invited me to share with you will help us to understand how. So, here is a brief German lesson for you.

"There are two German words for *you*, one of them formal and the other informal. The formal form, which is always capitalized, is *Sie*. The

146   **YOU AND WE**

informal form, which is what Buber used, is *du*.* Consequently, when Buber is talking about the *I-You* way, he is talking about the *I-Du* way, not the *I-Sie* way. Having lost any distinction between a formal and informal *you* in English,[32] this may seem insignificant to English speakers. However, Buber's choice to use *du* rather than *Sie* carries significant meaning in German and for his philosophy. Let me illustrate that with a relationship in this room.

"Let's suppose that Tim and I, here, barely know each other—which, it turns out, is really the case. When addressing each other, which German word do you suppose we would use—the informal *du* or the formal *Sie*?"

"*Sie?*"

"Yes, the formal *Sie* in that case. But what if we were to spend quite a lot of time together and became good friends? How would I address Tim *then*?"

"As *du*?" Zane answered.

Ricardo shook his head. "This is the point Dot was referring to that gets lost in translation. Whether I call another person *Sie* or *du* does not merely depend on how I see or experience them myself, in my mind. Whether I can begin calling another *du* depends on something outside of my own control, something that rests on the relationship itself: *I need the other person's permission.*

"Let me repeat that. Calling someone *du* is not my decision alone; *I need your permission to call you du.* Germans call that 'offering someone the *du.*'"

Zane found himself nodding in interest.

"There's a famous urban legend about this involving then-president Ronald Reagan and the German chancellor Helmut Kohl. After becoming friends, Chancellor Kohl is said to have offered the *du* to President Reagan by telling him, '*You can say you to me.*' While this sounds funny in English, it brings home a point that is obvious in the German

---

* *Sie* is pronounced *zee*; *du* is pronounced *doo*.

BUBER'S HYPHEN

language: Even the president of the United States couldn't decide on his own to call another *du*, no matter how he saw or felt toward Kohl. Kohl could become *du* to Reagan only with Kohl's permission. The word is an expression of a particular kind of mutual relationship."

Okay, that's starting to make sense, Zane thought. And then an insight flashed into his mind that pulled various strands of the conversation together. "So, are you saying that if all I'm doing is seeing someone else as a person, I'm actually objectifying them by making them into some idea of what a person is—an idea I'm carrying around in my head?"

"Yes, Zane, exactly. Without realizing it, we often conceptualize others in precisely that way. And when we do, our encounters with others happen in the psychologized version of the world we've created in our minds, which is a way of not really encountering others at all. But we don't realize this. We are caught in the same kind of illusion that this room creates. We think we are connected even though we are not."

"Ricardo, could I add something here?" Dot asked.

"By all means."

"If all of you think of your most lively, meaningful encounters," she said, "I bet you'll discover that they were times when you escaped your internal chatter and really connected with another, without expectation or script, without labels or judgments, and without posturing or pursuing an agenda. I'm thinking, for example, of the conversation Zane and I had late yesterday when I talked about how I'd been *blocking* in our relationship, and he spoke up and talked about how he'd been *breaking*. Do you all remember that?"

"Kind of unforgettable," Eliza said.

"That was an example of an *I-You* or *I-Du* moment," Dot said.

"Wait, what?" Zane said. "I'm confused. Why was that *I-You*? I don't remember giving you permission to call me *du*, by the way."

"Oh, but you did," Dot replied.

"Huh? How?"

"By the way you were so immediately present. You weren't hiding behind any masks, and you also weren't trying to manage impressions."

148   **YOU AND WE**

"You can say that again," Eliza said with a smirk.

Dot didn't blink. "You were fully there in that moment, Zane. You were as present as I've ever felt before. And that showed genuine respect for me—and for us. You weren't rehearsed, you weren't calculating, you were just there. And I didn't feel you trying to exert control over me or the conversation. You were open to whatever you encountered in me. You were there with me in the *between*. You were giving me your *du*. And I accepted it."

Zane thought about their exchange. It was true that all his internal chatter had quieted in that moment. He really *was* dialed in, and listening, and sharing. Out of the entire day, it had been the moment he felt most alive, surprising even himself by what he said. That was true. *So that's what it means to be I-You?*

"I want to come back to something Ricardo talked about a few minutes ago," Dot continued. "People think *I-You* is good and *I-It* is bad, but, as Ricardo explained, that isn't right. We live our lives in both ways, and necessarily so. We are, after all, thinking, analyzing beings. That fact is behind much of human innovation, and that part of us is *I-It*. We aren't fully present with others in those moments because we are so in our heads, but much good can come from serious thought. Thinking back on exchanges we've had with others is also something that happens in our heads and is therefore *I-It*, but that certainly doesn't mean it's bad. Buber recognized the benefits of both ways, not just the *I-You* way. However, I will say it again to be crystal clear: What *I-It* misses is relation— the *between*, the *with*, the *interhuman*. And if we pursue thought without connection, we end up losing what makes us uniquely us.

"Buber warned that if we tip too much toward *I-It* approaches, we do so at the expense of being able to truly connect. That puts us in dangerous territory. After all, machines can think—in many cases much faster and better than we can—and they're getting faster and smarter. But they can't *relate*. *I-You* is the exclusive territory of living beings, and we lose what is most unique and treasured about us if we encounter the world primarily in third person, as machines do, rather than second.

Second-person relational encounter should govern us, says British neuroscientist Iain McGilchrist in his fascinating body of work on the human brain,[33] with third-person seeing being utilized as a helpful tool in support. However, Western thinking has flipped this on its head. Nonrelational third-person seeing has become the modern world's default, even while we interact with others. We've bought in to experiencing life from this room.

"So, I thank you for showing up the way you did yesterday, Zane, and for respecting me enough to contend with me straightforwardly and openly. As I said yesterday, I just wish both of us had been able to do that three years ago. No telling what might have happened had we done so. Perhaps we would have made the same decisions. Or perhaps new and better options might have presented themselves. It certainly couldn't have made us worse off.

"But no matter now. The question for those of you from Bellweather is how you will meet each other from this time forward. You in Congress and those of you at PERC face the same question. How are you going to be with others? Are you going to stay in your own heads and continue to miss each other, or will you choose to let go of your concepts of each other, venture out, like Cree does amidst the trees, and start to truly encounter each other?"

She looked around at the group. "We've been going at it pretty intensely. Let's take a 30-minute break. Whatever else you do during these 30 minutes, I would invite you to connect with someone. Get out of your heads—out of your concepts, judgments, preconceptions, hang-ups, agendas, fears, and so on—and simply connect with someone. Meet them in the *between*. Maybe someone in this group, or maybe someone else.

"See you again in 30."

18

Breaking Open

Zane hadn't called Laney in weeks. As her phone rang, he started to feel this may not be a good idea. He was about to hang up when he heard her voice.

"Hello?"

That was the voice of the woman he had fallen in love with. They had met at Vanderbilt University during their freshman year in a swimming class they both dropped after the first session. Laney was from Lexington, Kentucky, where her father was an engineering professor. She went to Vanderbilt for its strong biomedical engineering program. Zane selected Vanderbilt because of the music scene in Nashville. He graduated with a degree in economics, but his main education was in songwriting and small stage performing up and down Nashville's Broadway Street over his years there.

The attraction between them was immediate. Laney was affable yet serious-minded. Zane was fun-loving and spontaneous—so much so that he was widely known by the nickname Zaney. He did well in school but put in little effort. He had gotten into drugs late in high school, and his addiction had landed him in rehab. As he spent far more time in Nashville's music venues than in class or on his studies, his lifestyle was high in potential for relapse. Two things kept him sober. First, his father had promised to cover all his educational costs so long as he stayed clean. But the second reason was ultimately his firewall: He didn't want to disappoint Laney. He had been open with her about his problems, and she was either at his side or on his mind whenever drugs were present. Which, in the circles he ran in, was often. She was straitlaced and religious. He was mostly agnostic, but he had faith in Laney, and she, for some reason, had faith in him. That, above all, kept him sober. Laney and Zaney married two weeks after graduation.

But that was a hundred thousand disappointments and arguments ago. Over the intervening years, their personalities had orbited around each other until they had almost switched places. Laney, who left biomedicine to run an art museum and studio, had become the fun and spontaneous one. Meanwhile, with every advancing year in his career, Zane had become more locked in and focused. Their conversations, once free-flowing and honest, had long ago become guarded and mechanical. They raised their kids together but had little else in common. She loved to travel and ended up doing it mostly with her friends. He mostly worked. His only outlet outside of work was golf, which he usually did alone. He still had his music, and a whimsical dream to one day write a musical that would run on the big Broadway stages in New York. But he'd long since given up any real hope of that. And he'd taken up drinking.

How does a relationship recover after more than two decades of neglect? How can you pull yourself out from under the weight of endless regrets? How can you forget the things that have been said to you, and the things you said back? What should you do when, notwithstanding all the accumulated pain, you still love the person who chooses to leave you?

After the empty closet announced that Laney had left, Zane set about trying to win her back. *Surely, she can't be serious*, he had thought. *We have problems, but doesn't everyone?* He built a strategic plan, the way his business-self had learned to do. He called her, frequently went over to the apartment she had rented in Georgetown, tried to talk her into giving marriage counseling another try, and wrote over a dozen songs for her. He tried to take her out to dinner, something they once enjoyed but had barely done in years, and he inundated her with messages.

In return? Nothing. Not a note, not a thank-you, not a word of encouragement, not a smile. Laney had gone cold. She told him, definitively, that they were over.

At first, Zane hadn't believed it, and he still pushed. But as their separation passed from weeks to months, and Laney continued to ignore or rebuff every effort he made at reconciliation, reality settled upon him like a dark cloud. He locked himself in his Alexandria home, rarely bothering to turn on the lights. He returned silence with silence. A bottle became his companion. Soon, it became the only thing that helped him wash out the pain.

In truth, he didn't know who he was without Laney and, either out of shame, desperate hope, or both, he did his best to maintain the facade to the outside that they were still together. No one at Bellweather knew they were separated. He suspected, now, that his kids might have an inkling, but he himself hadn't talked with them about it. His empty house, which he and Laney had only recently purchased and decorated together, mocked him.

Hearing her voice again sent a jolt through him like a charge of electricity. His heart jumped in his chest, and he was suddenly short of breath.

"Hi. How are you?" he said.

"I'm fine. And you?"

"Um, I'm okay."

She didn't say anything in response.

"I—um—I'm thinking about you."

"Zane, we've talked about this."

"No, I know, not that. I just—I just wanted to call and say hi. And to make sure you're okay."

"You don't think I can take care of myself?"

"No, Laney—no, I'm sorry, I didn't mean it like that. I guess I'm a little nervous." He chuckled oddly. "Can you believe that? So, no—I mean, I'm sorry. I really just wanted to say hi. That's all. And hearing your voice is nice."

The line was silent. Zane wondered if she'd hung up.

"It's good to hear your voice, too, Zane."

The words brought tears to his eyes. They meant so much and yet hurt so deeply. "Yeah . . ."

"I hope you are well," she followed up.

"Yeah, umm, I'm actually at this training thing up at Glenstone. Do you know it—the art museum up in Montgomery County?"

"Of course I know it. In fact, I know the owner and art director there."

"What? Really? How so?"

"The art world is pretty small, and she's a significant figure in it. Great person too."

Zane nodded. He wanted to say more, but the tears wouldn't let him.

"Why are you at a training at Glenstone? That sounds a little out of your wheelhouse."

Zane wiped his eyes. "Oh, it's not about art. You're not going to believe it. Dot Kessler is leading the training."

Laney didn't say anything for a moment. "That's probably uncomfortable for you. Is everything okay?"

"Yeah, everything's fine," he lied. "I'm good. The training's actually kind of interesting."

"Well, that's good. I'm happy to hear that. Listen, I have to go now, okay?"

"Oh, yeah, sure."

"Bye," she said.

"Bye—wait, Laney?"

She was gone.

Zane hunched over, tears spilling down his cheeks.

A few minutes later, he heard Dot calling from down the hall, announcing that they would be starting up again in a couple of minutes. He looked down at the note he was writing to Laney. It might be the last thing he would ever write her as her husband. He read through it again and penned a final sentence. Gathering his things, he left the room he had been using and walked toward the training room. *It's probably too late for us as a married couple*, he thought to himself, *but I'd at least like to learn how we can be friends again.*

"Welcome back, everyone," Dot greeted them. "I'm curious if there's anything you'd like to share. Anyone? Any experience that went especially well or especially poorly? Or somewhere in between?"

Sam raised his hand. "Eliza and I spent the break time together."

"Really? And how was it?"

"Really good, actually. I think I learned more about her in the last 30 minutes than I'd learned over the last decade in Congress together."

"And I told him that he must not have been listening all those years, because I'm a pretty open book." Eliza smiled mischievously.

"I think she's right; I haven't been listening. Only enough to try to obstruct and defeat her! But that isn't really listening, is it?"

"Well, you two seem to be in a pretty good place. *Why*, would you say?"

"Credit to Sam on that," Eliza said. "He came right over to me at the beginning of the break. Said something like, 'Eliza, I don't think I've given you a fair shake, or a fair hearing. If you don't mind, I'd just like to get to know you better. Don't worry about the politics—that's not what this is about. You're a super interesting person, and I'd just like to learn more about you.'"

"I think you added that 'super interesting person' bit," Sam said with a laugh.

"I might have. But I know you were thinking it."

Everyone laughed. "It sounds like you had a great conversation!" Dot said.

"It was a start," Eliza replied.

156   **YOU AND WE**

"Yes," Sam agreed. "I hope it was just a beginning."

"And would you characterize your conversation as being *I-It* or *I-You?*" Dot asked.

"*I-You,*" Sam said.

"Eliza?"

"I'm not sure. Maybe some of both?"

"Fair enough. Anyone else like to share something?"

Arlo raised his hand. "I guess this is Congress Day," he said. "Dex and I met too."

"Hmm, and?"

"And can I just say that I like this man? He's a good soul."

"I agree," Dot said. "He is. But what if he wasn't? What would be different for you, Arlo?"

"Hmm, I don't know for sure. Maybe we wouldn't have talked."

"Would that have been a helpful solution—helpful for the country, in your case?"

He shook his head. "Probably not, no."

"So, what if he *was* a tough and difficult person—like some of your colleagues in the Senate probably are? What have you learned that might guide you in that case?"

"Well, I think, first of all, that I have to find a way out of this room, so to speak, you know? It's really easy to put labels on others, or to place them in categories. And when you do that, you almost don't need to talk with them anymore since you think you already know them. But that's just because you've loaded a rendition of them into your head. That's the *psychologizing the world* point you made earlier. That really hit me. I think I do that a lot. Even with people that I love."

"And when we do that," Dot replied, "we think we're out there with the trees even though we haven't even left the room. Isn't that right?"

"Exactly. And the way it goes down in Congress is that I'm not alone in the room. I'm with a whole bunch of other people who believe pretty much how I do, and we look out at others with unified talking points

BREAKING OPEN 157

and labels. So, it's not just me that's seeing them that way—everyone is thinking it! You know what I mean?"

Dot nodded. "So, you *bond* with each other and *break* and *block* toward others. *Bridging* and *expanding* remain out of reach."

"It's not so much that they remain out of reach as that I don't even think about them. Who would ever want to bridge *toward*, or expand *with*, people like *them*?"

"Which is likely what they're thinking as well—about *you*."

"Undoubtedly. And now you have a picture of what Congress is like nowadays."

"So, what are you and Dex going to do about that?"

"We're going to keep talking—stay in the *between* with each other, rather than in our own heads and narratives. One of the things we discussed is that there are no narratives in the *between*. By that I mean that we aren't living by a script we want to be true of us and to have acknowledged by others. There is dialogue and conversation, but we aren't playing out stories. The moment we start worrying about that, we're right back in this room."

"On that note," Dex chimed in, "something else we discussed was how it would help to stay focused on our levels of relation with others, rather than on the difficulty of particular persons or groups. Difficult or not, our *relationship* is still at a particular level. If we can stay focused on trying to raise that up a level or two, we're thinking that might keep us engaged and away from the trap of spinning self-serving narratives about ourselves and others, which is what we do from inside this room. Especially when we're dealing with people we're experiencing as difficult."

Dot nodded. "I like all of that, Dex and Arlo. Very much. Thank you. Anyone else want to share something?"

Rita raised her hand. "Three of us from Bellweather huddled during the break—me, Judy, and Cree."

"Zane as well?"

"No, I was on the phone with someone else."

"Very good. So, what did the three of you talk about, Rita?"

"Well, we talked about one of the big challenges we have in the company, which is that everyone feels like they're being judged and evaluated for their outlooks or mindsets. After you left, the company focused its whole leadership approach around that. But you can't really know what someone's internal attitude really is since it's *inside* them. So, no one else is really positioned to judge, you know? But this focus on who we are on the inside is driving two terrible things in the company: weaponization and hypocrisy. People feel judged and criticized for 'not having the right attitude about people,' so they're faking what they think their leaders want to see. And then those same leaders, while making decisions that have harsh consequences for people, put on an act like they're deeply concerned about them. It's a charade in every direction, and we all feel it. Bellweather always prided itself on its culture. But now it feels like the so-called culture company broke its culture."

"I'm sad to hear that," Dot said. "Do you have a perspective on this, Zane? Do you agree with what Rita is saying?"

In truth, Zane was only half-listening. His mind still lingered on his phone call with Laney. What he had heard didn't surprise him, though, as Mikél Dunning had been making similar points in their one-on-ones recently. "I guess I'd like to hear more," he said. "Given what we've been talking about here, if we're driving people into their heads to make it seem like their hearts are right, we're on the wrong path. I'm open to doing whatever we need to do to change that."

"Do you really mean that?" Rita asked. "Or is that just more feel-good talk?"

Zane took a deep breath—a centering breath. "No, I mean it. Although I'm not exactly sure what to do about it, to be honest. Dot and Ricardo have kind of dismantled much of what I thought I knew. But I'm open.

"Besides," he said, "I have bigger problems."

Dot looked at him. "Do you want to talk about it?"

He thought about it. Should he share what he was going through? Would it be right in this setting? And would it be right by Laney? Or his children? "No, I don't think so," he finally said. "I just have some things to figure out."

"You and me both, Zane," Dot replied.

"And me," Eliza said.

"And me."

"Same here."

"And me."

"Me too."

"And me."

"And me."

"Same for me."

"Me too."

"And me."

"Me, too, for sure."

"And me."

"It sounds like we all have company," Dot said.

As Zane looked around the room, he felt something new. He was grateful for these people.

19

Connecting

"Zane mentioned bigger problems," Ricardo said, "and we all have them, don't we? Let me tell you about a time recently when some of my problems were obvious to everyone.

"I was up in Baltimore at Johns Hopkins University on behalf of the task force. It was my first solo run sharing some of the ideas we all have been exploring. It was just me with a group of 20 or so leaders. Until Dot walked in just before we got started.

"Have any of you ever had to make a presentation in front of someone whose opinion mattered to you terribly?"

Everyone nodded.

"Well, one year ago, in that workshop, Dot's opinion mattered to me more than anyone else's in the world. And I was a disaster. My first big mistake was worrying what she was thinking. My second was doing last-minute preparation and going over my presentation rather than getting to know the people in the group.

"As a result, I started the morning in a most impersonal way—referring to people with pronouns rather than names, worrying about what Dot was thinking, and getting more and more in my own head as the energy in the room seemed low and the interest lower. I was becoming more anxious by the minute."

"I don't buy it," Eliza said. "I don't see you as the nervous type."

"You don't know me very well, Eliza, but thank you. I actually get really anxious in front of people."

"But you teach in a university!"

"As little as I can get away with!" Ricardo said. "I mostly focus on my research and writing. About electrons and quarks. People terrify me!"

"Really? I never would have guessed it."

"I've learned a lot over the last year," he replied. "I don't lock myself in this room like I used to. But I was locked in without a key the morning of that workshop. In fact, when Dot and I went to lunch after the train wreck of that morning, she said it was the worst workshop she'd ever seen. Don't deny it!" he said, pointing at Dot. "That's what you said!"

"Oh, I won't deny it," Dot replied with a laugh. "It really was! But that was mostly on me. I threw you off. But you can't leave it there, Ricardo. You have to share what happened in the afternoon, when it became one of the most *powerful* workshops I've ever seen."

He nodded and turned on the screen again. "There's something we need to think about in order to understand what changed."

CLOSED OFF OR BREAKING OPEN

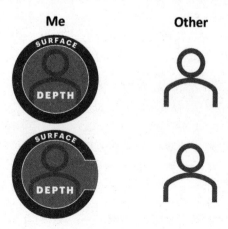

CONNECTING 163

"Imagine that the person on the left of these two diagrams is you. What is different between these versions of you?"

"In the top version, I'm closed off," Rita said. "And in the bottom version, it looks like there is an opening into my interior."

Ricardo nodded. "What do you think that opening means?"

Rita thought about it. "Well, maybe it means that I allow others to reach me—to touch or move me, or that I allow myself to consider others. Something like that?"

"That is well said, Rita. Thank you. The French philosopher Gabriel Marcel says that achieving this depends on our maintaining an openness to others that he calls *availability*. One who is available to others, he says, 'keeps the doors of his soul ajar.'[34]

"Does anyone else have ideas to add to Rita's insights?"

Sam raised his hand. "I'm not sure it's as much about letting others in as letting myself out."

"Say more about that," Ricardo invited.

"I'm thinking that this wall we keep around ourselves not only keeps others at a distance but also keeps ourselves locked in. So, the top diagram is a picture of me in this room, for example, with a barrier between myself and others. While it's true that that barrier keeps the trees from coming in to meet me, as it were, it also keeps me from going out to meet them. Our surfaces touch on either side of the barrier, but we don't connect—mostly because I'm not stepping out to join them."

"Very interesting insight, Sam. Thank you."

To the group, he asked, "What would you all say is the difference between what this graphic is calling our *surface* and our *depth*?"

Pam raised her hand. "It reminds me of the individual side of the four quadrants diagram from yesterday. *Surface* in that case might refer to what others can see about us—our behaviors, for example, our words, gestures, and so on. *Depth* would then mean our attitudes—our beliefs, for example, mindsets, worries, hopes, objectives, fears, and so on."

"I would maybe add that *surface* could also include not only what others can see in us but also what we *want* them to see in us," Eliza added. "We're trying to make a certain impression on other people—like we do on social media, for example. Or in politics, for that matter. So, our surface is what we are presenting to others."

"What would our *depth* refer to in that case?" Ricardo asked.

"I think it's getting at what is real in us—not necessarily who we want others to think we are but who we really are. It would include all the things Pam just mentioned—our real attitudes, for example, beliefs, worries, and so on. And the actual human beneath them."

Ricardo nodded. "Yes. Buber made a similar point. He talked about two different kinds of people—*image people*, who interact from what you just described as our surfaces, and *being people*, who interact and connect from their interiors or depths.[35] While we can *interact* with others from the surface, we can *connect* only when we operate from depth. When we're acting from a surface level, we're concerned with *seeming* a certain way, just as you said—seeming to be an interesting person, perhaps, or smart, funny, thoughtful, impressive, successful, and so on. Or, on other occasions, seeming to be powerless or innocent. We are trying to make a particular impression, or else to hide a particular trait we want others not to know about us. We are self-concerned, protected, managed, promotional, and emotionally distant."

Zane started thinking about how much of his life was driven by *seeming*. His shame over his failed marriage, for example, which had caused him to avoid dealing with the difficulties between himself and Laney over the years and that now caused him to try to keep their separation and imminent divorce secret. Or his attempts to live up to his father's reputation, or to escape Dot's shadow. His worries over these two days about how others might be viewing him. His reticence to let anyone listen to the music he had written out of fear of what they would think. And the ways he tried to manage every professional conversation.

The more he thought about it, the more he could see that *seeming* had crept in and come to dominate almost every facet of his life. *Where do I operate from* being *rather than* seeming? He honestly couldn't think of an area of his life that hadn't become infested with *seeming*. Even the coldness he had shown toward Laney since she had rebuffed his attempts to reconcile was part of *seeming*: He couldn't let her know how hurt he was. And then he realized that this had started years before she moved away. He hid his feelings from her and covered his hurt. He closed himself off to minimize the pain he felt, a move that only exacerbated both the pain and the separation. *I left her before she left me*, he suddenly realized. *I moved out before she did!*

"One way to understand these illustrations," Ricardo continued, "is that they are partial forms of the *I-It* and *I-You* diagrams we discussed earlier. In the top diagram, I am locked inside myself, interacting with others but not moved by them. The depth of my being is covered by a shell that insulates me from others and keeps them out of my formative depths. In the lower diagram, that surface shell is breaking open. As you all have said, I'm letting myself out and others in. I am beginning to offer my *du*.

"Now, here is my question for you: Which of these is a diagram of me during that morning workshop I butchered?"

"It sounds like the top one," Eliza said. "But I'm still not sure I buy it."

Ricardo chuckled. "Buy it or not, I was definitely the top diagram that morning."

"But you have to share what happened in the afternoon," Dot repeated.

"I think it would be better if you recounted it, Dot. As a participant that day, your perspective would likely be more helpful to the group than mine."

"Okay. Then I'll start with what happened when we went to lunch." She turned toward the group. "As we ate, Ricardo unfolded himself to me. He shared about his anxiety, his embarrassment, how he felt he had let the group and me down, how he wasn't sure he was cut out to do this, how he didn't know how to move forward in the afternoon given how terrible the morning had been, how some challenges in his life were getting in his way as well, and so on. He was real, he was open, he was unsure, he was searching. And wow, I could have listened to him that way for hours—he was so open, so real, so powerfully and fully present.

"What then transpired after lunch was one of the most miraculous turnarounds I have ever witnessed. Ricardo started the post-lunch session by opening up to the group about his own experience that morning. He acknowledged that although he'd been trying to teach them about the workings of human connection, he had completely cut himself off from them. He apologized for violating everything he had been sharing with them.

"As he talked, I looked around the room. The same thing that had happened with me over lunch was happening with them. The very people who just an hour earlier hadn't been able even to meet his gaze were leaning forward in their chairs, their eyes riveted on him. The room was alive. *They* were alive.

"How can you explain that shift? What changed from the morning to the afternoon?"

"Ricardo showed up in the afternoon as the lower diagram," Pam said. "He was breaking open."

"Yes," Dot agreed. "And that created the opportunity for this to happen . . .

GENUINE MEETING

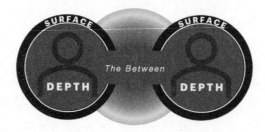

"This is a diagram of two people who are breaking open toward each other—people who are showing up in the way illustrated in the lower of the two diagrams Ricardo was just showing us. Metaphorically, one of

CONNECTING 167

these people might be *hydrogen* and the other *oxygen*. Their goal is not to convert the other to themselves. It is rather to enter into relation—that is, *with difference*."

Everyone studied the image for a moment.

Cree raised his hand. "I have a couple questions."

"Of course. Go ahead."

"The surface areas around the people in this diagram are thinner than in the earlier images you showed us, or else their interiors are larger, or both," he said. "Is that inadvertent or on purpose? And, if on purpose, what are you saying by that?"

"That's incredibly perceptive of you, Cree. That very subtle change is intentional. Since others enter our depths when we connect, our concerns are no longer only about ourselves. We *expand* in the way we discussed yesterday. Our selves expand and we get larger, and we've tried to illustrate that by expanding the interiors on this diagram. This is what we call *the first sign of connection*—that we ourselves somehow change, whether by gaining a new thought, deeper appreciation, a new perspective, or feel touched or moved in some way by someone else, even if we don't agree with them. *Our interiors expand and grow larger*."

"How about the expanding circle around what you're calling *the between*?" Cree followed up. "What does that signify?"

"This is another facet of *expanding* and has to do with *the second sign of connection*. But let me mention a few things about *the between* first, and then I'll address your question about the expanding circle. Fair enough?"

Cree nodded.

"What is this space between us, as depicted on this diagram? To consider that question, let's ponder communication for a moment. If you think about it, every communication is three-dimensional. It has an *outside*, an *inside*, and a *between*.

"The *outside* of a communication refers to its content—the words that are used, the concepts that are shared, and how these are delivered. The *inside* refers to the person's interior or soul, which is part of every communication, whether authentically or not, and whether or not intended. The *between* refers to the interplay between communication partners, or, in a group setting, between a speaker and their audience. It's what people sense as *energy*. A conversation or room can be alive, or it can be dead. That energy or mutuality, or its lack, is the realm of the between.

"So, when we interact, you can't capture the whole of the experience by considering only what's happening within me and within you. Life can't be reduced merely to psychology. There is also what is happening *between* us. This is the realm of *the between*.

"When we open ourselves to each other in the way depicted in this diagram, the participants in this mutual relationship are no longer just presenting their surfaces to each other but allowing each other into their depths. Gabriel Marcel calls this *communion*. He says that true communion happens only between people who are mutual *subjects* with each other, a point he emphasizes by calling this phenomenon by another name as well: *the intersubjective*[36]—which implies, I think, that the presence of the other is not only *over there* for me anymore, but also in my depths. 'In an essential relation,' Buber said, 'the barriers of the individual being are in fact breached and a new phenomenon appears.'[37] He called this, as you know, *I-You* or *I-Du relation*. He also called it *the interhuman space*.[38]

"Which brings us, Cree, to your question about the expanding circle. Not limited to what is going on within my head or yours, neither of us owns or possesses the relation. Like a good improv skit, it takes on a life of its own. Something new is born—something more and different from either of us. Buber called it *leaping fire*.[39] The emergence of this convergent offspring is *the second sign of connection*. It is a phenomenon that would have been nonexistent and therefore inaccessible alone. It's the birth of something new out of the union of difference. It's what becomes possible beyond *bridging*, and it's what I saw happening during the afternoon of Ricardo's workshop at Johns Hopkins."

"That's what *water* is," Pam spoke up. "It's the convergent offspring of hydrogen and oxygen coming together. It's the evidence that they opened themselves to each other."

"Yes, Pam," Dot said. "Thank you for tying that together for us. When we bring our differences and open ourselves to each other, we enter the interhuman space where we can make water."

"Or *TNT*."

It was Stuart Reddy, PERC's Chief Engineer, who had been silent and withdrawn until that moment.

"Stuart!" Dot exclaimed. "It's good to hear from you!"

He didn't respond to the welcome.

Dot filled the silence. "I'm sorry. Could you repeat what you said?"

"You keep talking about the merits of making water, but you can bring atoms together in ways that produce a whole range of things, including terribly dangerous compounds. Hydrogen peroxide, for example, which can be harmful in some applications, is made from two atoms each of hydrogen and oxygen. Or, to take the compound I mentioned, a single molecule of TNT is made up of seven atoms of carbon, five atoms of hydrogen, three atoms of nitrogen, and six atoms of oxygen. You put them together and *boom*! Relation isn't necessarily such a great thing."

"That's an important observation, Stuart. It points to a potential confusion we haven't addressed clearly enough. That confusion is around the words *relationship* and *relation*. Relation*ships* are what we build with each other. However, *relation*, by contrast, is simply a fact of existence. Relation isn't built; it's already there—a reality, not a construct. Everything is in relation, including us, so we are in relation whether we want it or not, and whether we have a relationship or not. But you are right to say that certain kinds of *relationships* can produce negative outcomes. After all, as we've discussed, there are different levels of relationships, from the quite negative to the sublime. And while we might say a *compounding* relationship is great, it's also true that a *division*-level relationship can be really negative—downright explosive, in fact, to extend your metaphor."

170 YOU AND WE

"To prevent explosions, sometimes it's better to keep things apart," Stuart said, expressionless.

Dot nodded. "I'd agree with that. Sometimes that *is* best. At work, for example, some people's contributions might disrupt the relational field of an organization so negatively that it's necessary to let them go. And setting boundaries can be an illustration of that point as well. So, yes, I would agree with you, Stuart. However, we need also to be clear-eyed about what we are giving up when we choose to keep ourselves or others closed off: We are foreclosing the possibility of connection, and the *compounding* and *expansion* that can come with it. We are choosing not to explore the potentialities of the *between* and are rather opting for the shallows of the lower levels of relation in those cases, and that will have to be good enough. If we want more than that, however, we will have to break open."

Stuart didn't say anything, and Dot paused for a moment, thinking.

"Stuart, your comments are calling to mind an experience I had over two decades ago, after I left Bellweather—a time when I chose separation, just as you are suggesting."

"Wait, you left Bellweather more than 20 years ago?" Eliza asked. "I thought it had only been three years."

"I left Bellweather twice, and what I'm thinking about now is a conversation I had with Zane's father nearly 25 years ago.

"After he fired me."

20

Differences Coming Together

"Zane's father, Frank Savage, was a tough boss," Dot began. "Would you agree with that, Zane?"

"Believe me, you don't know the half of it."

Dot laughed. "Undoubtedly not! Frank was amazing, but over my first decade at Bellweather, it felt like he was always breathing down my neck and getting in everyone's business. He grew into a different person and leader later, but early on we had some tough times. The higher I climbed in the company, the more autonomy I felt I had earned, but the less, it felt, he gave me. I grew so fed up with him over a period of years that I ultimately put in my notice. He promptly fired me on the spot and had me escorted out of the building, treating me like a traitor. And I wasn't the only one. He lost half of his executive team in less than a month. It's like you were saying, Stuart—we all felt we needed separation from him, not connection. And his reaction was to separate from us even harder."

Stuart nodded slightly.

"I thought that was the end of my story with Bellweather. Until Frank showed up on my doorstep two months later.

"What he said to me probably won't make sense to you without a bit more context. You see, despite his successes in business, Frank was struggling in his family life, and he was releasing the pressure he was feeling there in all his interactions at work. In the year or so before I left, one of the things challenging him—and therefore us—the most was his relationship with his youngest son."

Zane was listening intently now, as memories of that time rushed back to his mind. He wondered if everyone had deduced that *he* was that youngest son.

"I was stunned when I answered the door and saw Frank standing there. He was literally the last person I would have expected at my house. I didn't think he even knew where I lived.

"'Frank?' I exclaimed in surprise.

"'Hi, Dot,' he said. 'Would it be okay if I came in?'

"I wasn't comfortable with that and suggested we sit out on the porch instead.

"'You're probably wondering why I'm here,' he said.

"'Yeah, you might say that,' was my reply.

"He said, 'I owe you a massive apology, Dot. I don't expect you to accept it, but I have to offer it all the same. My whole life is falling to pieces, and I'm only just now beginning to see my role in all the turmoil.'

"I was skeptical, to say the least. I had heard from former colleagues that things were going poorly at the company, and I viewed this as a desperate effort by Frank to get his financial house back in order. He had been successful in his life not only because of his smarts and his work ethic, but also because he could ingratiate himself with others when necessary. I wasn't going to fall for it. I wasn't interested.

"'Well, I'm glad to hear you're starting to see things with more clarity, Frank,' I told him.

"And then we fell into a prolonged, uncomfortable silence. He just sat looking across the street into the woods on the other side. I don't

DIFFERENCES COMING TOGETHER

know how long we sat there like that. It felt like 10 minutes, although it was perhaps only a couple.

"'I can't do this alone, Dot,' he finally said. 'I don't have confidence in my intuitions or my decisions anymore. I need someone I trust— someone who will stand up to me with their own convictions and who will be able to consider mine even when I'm being the hardcore pain in the ass I too often am. I'd like to be able to moderate that part of myself, and I'm working on it, believe me, but I'm also a realist. By the time you get to be my age, a lot of it is baked in.'

"In all our years working together, I'd never heard Frank say anything quite like that. I'd never heard him admit failure. I'd never heard him question himself as he was then doing, even though he was still giving himself a bit of a pass with the idea that he was too old to change. *Is this an act?* I wondered. Still not feeling completely safe, I kept my guard up.

"'You said you wanted to apologize, but I don't think I've heard one yet,' I said.

"He didn't reply for a moment. 'You're right,' he finally said. 'Old habits, I suppose.'

"There it was—another excuse. I stood up, offered him my hand, and said, 'Thanks for coming by, Frank.'

"And then I saw something I had never seen in Frank Savage. A tear was collecting on his lid and beginning to spill over onto his cheek. He was clearly dealing with burdens that went way beyond the two of us. It was a crack in what I now recognize had been a well-managed shell."

I never saw him cry, Zane thought. *Not even once.*

"I slowly sat back down.

"'You're the smartest person I've ever worked with, Dot,' he said. 'And I admire how you are with people. You're way better with people than I am.'

"'That's not really saying much,' I replied."

Zane erupted in laughter. "You told my old man *that*? Wow, that took some courage!"

"Yes, but by then I knew your father was someone who appreciated direct talk."

"Did he in *this* case?" Zane asked.

"He actually burst out laughing, kind of like you just did. Only he kept laughing on and off for the next 20 minutes or so. He kept recalling times when he had totally botched up an interaction with someone. The memories came to him in waves, and he just kept telling me story after story after story, incredulous at his own ridiculousness.

"I think it was cathartic for him in a way, and I felt myself opening up a bit as well. But he still hadn't apologized to me for anything.

"'So, Frank,' I said, 'are you going to apologize to me for something specific, or are you just going to add that failure to your list of stories?'

"And boy did he ever roar at that! 'You're right! I haven't even apologized yet!' he exclaimed, slapping his leg. 'Can you believe that!' Another wave of laughter rolled through his body. He was like a man drunk on the hilarity of his own mistakes who was awakening with wonder to a different kind of life. It was a remarkable thing to witness.

"Then, all of a sudden, he said he needed to get me something from the car. He returned to my porch with a book, which he extended to me. 'I believe you have been looking for this,' he said.

"Sure enough, it was a book I had misplaced six months or so prior. I'd looked all over for it. It was my copy of *The Silmarillion*, by J. R. R. Tolkien. It was Tolkien's deep backstory for the entire *Lord of the Rings* world and cosmos, and the margins were filled with my notes trying to put all the pieces of that universe together in ways I could remember. I kept the book at work because I would dive into it on occasion when I had a few minutes' break and needed to clear my head. Being something of a Tolkien geek, losing it with all my notes really shook me.

"I asked him where he'd found it.

"And then he said, 'I didn't find it, Dot. I took it. And I am *so* sorry! It's completely inexcusable.'

"I said, 'What? You *took* it? What do you mean? Why?'

DIFFERENCES COMING TOGETHER 175

"He pointed at the chair he had been sitting in and asked, 'Do you mind if I sit down and tell you about it?'

"I didn't know what to say and just extended my hand to invite him to sit again.

"'I've been searching myself for why I did it,' he said. 'How does someone get to a place where that's even a possibility—to do something that ridiculous and juvenile?' He shook his head pathetically. 'Seriously, I'm so sorry. So why did I take it? I think there were two reasons, with the first being mostly a pitiful excuse for the second. I'll start with the pitiful excuse: I'd seen you reading the book around the company at times, and that irked me.'

"'Did you think I was reading on company time or something?' I asked. 'That's crazy. And, by the way, taking the book would have been ridiculous even *had* I been reading it on company time!'

"'I couldn't agree more,' he replied. 'Which is why I said it was just an excuse for my real motivation. The biggest reason, I think, is that I've been jealous of you, Dot. Stealing your book was a small way of hurting you for my own insecurities.'

"'*Jealous* of me?' I exclaimed. 'Why would *you*, Frank Savage, be jealous of *me*? In comparison to you, I've barely done anything with my life.'

"'First of all, that isn't at all true, and you know it,' he said. 'If you were to ask anyone in the company why I might be jealous of you, do you think they'd have a difficult time coming up with reasons?' He laughed resignedly. 'There are lots of reasons why I could be jealous of you, but the biggest is that people *like* you. They want more of Dot Kessler. They trust you. They follow you. They respond to you with enthusiasm. In my own company, people were gravitating more to you than to me, and I felt threatened by that.'"

This comment disquieted Zane. He, too, had effectively fired Dot. And why? *Because of how highly everyone thought of her.*

No, that's not right, he argued with himself. *She had to go because of how she took the spotlight for herself rather than keeping it brightly and deservedly on my father and the company. That's a different thing entirely!* But another internal voice, although faint, said, *Is that really the truth? Did she really desire the spotlight, or were people naturally attracted to her because she didn't care about it? Maybe it's someone* else *who craves the spotlight.*

Dot's voice pulled Zane back to the story. "Then Frank asked me something that ended up changing the course of my life. 'I'm sorry about the book,' he said, 'and I'm sorry as well that I had you escorted out of the building. I should have listened to your reasons for wanting to leave and tried to begin rectifying them right then. I know you've moved on, which I totally understand. But I couldn't live with myself if I didn't come to see you—first to apologize for being a jackass, and also to ask if you wouldn't consider coming back.'

"I told him I was starting a new job the very next week.

"'I know,' he replied. 'But I think you'd be better off at Bellweather.'

"I reminded him that it hadn't ended well for me the first time and asked why I should return simply because of what he was then saying.

"He let out a long exhale. 'You probably shouldn't,' he said. 'But before you entirely dismiss it,' he added, 'I wonder if you would do two things.'

"I told him that would depend on what they were.

"'First of all,' he said, 'I'd like your help thinking through how we could create an entirely different culture in the company. You have insights, perspectives, and experience that I don't, and I think I have some things you don't have either. If we put our minds and hearts to it, I think we could create an approach to leadership and work that would be transformational in the business and that would help me to stay inside the lines of acceptable behavior.

"'And secondly,' he said, 'I'd invite you to call my son. Maybe more than anyone else, he's probably the person who could help you to see whether I'm just *talking* about changing or if I'm serious about it.'"

Zane had forgotten about that phone call. It had struck him as odd at the time. Although he had met Dot once or twice at his dad's office,

DIFFERENCES COMING TOGETHER

he barely knew her. And besides, how many 19-year-olds are given by their father as a character reference? He remembered Dot saying that his father had suggested she call him. "Why?" he had asked. "I'm not exactly sure," she had replied. "I think he feels he's been unjustifiably hard on you, and he's wondering if you would ever be able to forgive him."

Zane then told her about the reunion they had just had, and how they had apologized to each other for all the pain they had caused. He told her about how Frank had owned all of it and pledged to become the loving father Zane had not yet had. And how Zane believed him.

Dot asked why he believed him, and Zane had replied: "Because, say what you want about my dad, but he always does what he says he'll do."

Dot's voice pulled Zane back to the moment. "Obviously, since I went back to Bellweather, you know what I ultimately decided. And Frank, as always, was as good as his word. We continued to open ourselves more and more to each other, and the space between us gave birth to the most robust and powerful leadership and team training program either of us had ever encountered. Neither of us could have produced it alone, and it became far more than the sum of our individual contributions. Looking back on my career, riding that creative wave with Frank was one of my most cherished times."

Zane reflected proudly on Bellweather's leadership training curriculum—*Bellweather Leadership*, as it was called—which he had extensively revised after Dot's departure. He had heard whisperings around the company about his changes. Reasoning that the changes were made as much to erase Dot from memory as for any other reason, with full-throated irony, employees had taken to calling it *Lead Like a Savage*.

"As I look back on that conversation on my porch," Dot continued, "and then on all the work that Frank and I did together over the succeeding years, what strikes me is how Frank offered me his *du*. I wasn't yet offering mine at that point. When he showed up at my door, I was all closed up."

"For good reason!" Eliza said.

"Yes, perhaps for good reason. And, Stuart, perhaps you would agree with that too."

He nodded. "Yes, I would."

"But by offering his *du*—by showing up as depicted on that lower diagram Ricardo showed us—he invited me to meet him in the *between*."

"How did my dad offer his *du*?" Zane asked.

"In four ways."

21

Offering Your *Du*

Remember what Ricardo taught us about the meaning of *I-You* or *I-Du?*" Dot said. "In *I-You* relation, others become a *du* for us, and this can happen only if they offer us their *du*. We cannot make someone our *du*—whether through trying to see them in a particular way or through any other artifice. *Du* is not, and can never be, an object of my perception. So, *I-You* is not simply a matter of seeing others in a particular way but is rather a relationship where we mutually break through the barriers around us that keep us from being moved in fundamental ways by each other.

"I want to share with you four elements that characterize offering one's *du*, and we each can consider not only how Frank showed up for me in those ways but also the degree to which these elements capture how we have been with each other over our time together. Fair enough?"

Everyone nodded.

"The first element is what we were talking about earlier—*allowing difference, differentiation, or space between us.*[40] In an *I-You* relationship, two beings engage with each other as fully independent and whole.

Buber calls this being *independent opposites*,[41] and it's what he means by there being space between us. If we experience others only in terms of ourselves and our own perspectives, projects, or desires, there is no space between us, which makes true relation impossible.

"With this idea in mind, let me give you a scenario, and you tell me whether there is space in it.

"I'm with a colleague, and I want to help him see how he's mistaken about something. To prepare my best arguments, I study up on his position before we meet. During our meeting, I listen to his arguments and then try to show him what he is missing.

"Now, is there space between me and my colleague in this scenario?"

"That's all there is to the situation?" Zane asked. "It's not much of a story at all."

"I agree, Zane, it isn't. And why not? What makes the story so small?"

Rita raised her hand. "I think it's because it's only about *you*."

"Yes, Rita. Say more about that."

"Well, there's not much to say. The scenario is about you from start to finish. You have an opinion you think is right, you think your colleague is therefore wrong in his different opinion, and you're trying to help him see things as you do. There isn't even another person in that story. It's just about you."

"So, is there space between myself and my colleague in this case? Is he an *other* who stands apart and opposite from me?"

"Not at all. He exists only in terms of you."

"Exactly right. And for that reason, there is no real relation here. There is no other to whom I can offer my *du*.

"Now, contrast that with this. A friend of Buber's set up a meeting in London between Buber and the poet T. S. Eliot. When Buber was asked whether he found his opinions to be different from Eliot's, Buber said, 'When I meet a man, I am not concerned with opinions but with the man.' Now, how is the scenario Buber describes different from the one I described?"

OFFERING YOUR *DU*

"You were *only* concerned with opinions," Stuart answered, "not with the man."

"Yes, Stuart. And which approach has space in it?"

"Buber's."

"Very good. Buber's approach gives him a partner to whom he can offer his *du*, whereas my approach allows no otherness. 'Only when every means has collapsed,' he wrote, 'does the meeting come about.'[42]

"Now, let's think about Frank's example. Did he allow space between us? Did he engage with me as a fully independent opposite? Or had he collapsed our differences by making me a means to his end?"

"The only reason he was on your doorstep was to convince you to come back," Stuart said.

"I don't think that's true," Pam replied. "He was there because he had done Dot wrong, and he knew it. He wanted to apologize to her, even though it took him a while to do it!"

"To the point of whether you were a fully *independent opposite* to him," Sam spoke up, "I think it's clear that you were. He recognized that you had strengths he didn't have, and he also thought you had every reason not to return. He wouldn't have blamed you for that at all. I think it's true, as Stuart said, that he hoped you would return, but I didn't sense any manipulation in what he said or did. He allowed all the space in the world."

"That's what it felt like to me," Dot agreed. "That meeting on my porch was perhaps the first time I felt that space when interacting with Frank. Before that, I was a person in his life, not a person with my own life."

Laney's words came to Zane's mind again: *You don't care about anything or anyone but yourself.* He had dismissed her comment out of hand because it was obvious to him how much he cared about others—about the kids, for example, and many of the people at work. But he suddenly realized that he'd misunderstood what she was saying. Her point wasn't that he didn't care about others; it was rather that his caring about others

182   YOU AND WE

was always *in terms of himself.* He didn't allow space between others and himself—*that's* what she was saying.

Is that true? he wondered. He quickly canvassed his relationships—with Laney, Jackson, Allison, his father, and his mother, who had passed away years earlier. He thought about his relationships with Dot, Ricardo, Judy, Rita, and Cree. He thought about Mikél Dunning, and about his friend Hal. He looked around at the people in the room. *Have I been encountering them as independent opposites, or are all these relationships in terms of what they mean for me?* He thought about the story Dot told about his father coming to her home. *Have I ever been the version of my father that apologized to Dot that day?* He looked at Dot—both with the history between them in mind but also as a proxy for everyone else in his life. His gaze fell to his hands on his lap, and he shook his head very slightly. *I'm not sure I've ever been that person.*

"So, again," Dot continued, "to offer your *du*, you must have someone who is fully *other* to whom you can offer it—someone who is fully unique and distinct, not captured in an understanding or desire within your head but standing completely apart from you. So, the first thing that must be present to offer another your *du* is distance or space. We don't experience the other in our heads; we encounter them directly, our own personal uniqueness entering into relation with their personal uniqueness. It is across that space that we offer our *du*.

"A second element of offering one's *du* has to do with status—namely, that there is no difference in status when one utters *du*. Extending your *du* is a horizontal act. There is no higher or lower or better or worse in *I-Du* or *I-You* relation. Status, which is a mental construct anyway, melts away. We don't hover over others, judging them from what some people call a *one-up position*. And, by the same token, we don't cower beneath them, judging ourselves from a *one-down position*. We also don't keep ourselves removed from them, with an air of objective superiority. We learn from everyone and have things to offer as well, whether we're senior or junior, higher-ranking, or lower. We join with others—horizontally, on the level, human-with-human, subject-with-subject.

OFFERING YOUR *DU* 183

"Think about Frank. When he came to my home, did he approach me in a *one-up* or *one-down* way, or was his approach horizontal?"

"In some ways, it sounds like he was almost *one-down*," Judy answered. "But in other ways, the whole conversation felt horizontal."

"I want to understand what sounded *one-down* to you, Judy," Dot followed up. "Was it because he was feeling like he needed to apologize?"

"No, it was more that he thought you were better than him in a lot of ways."

"Oh, I get what you're saying. Yes, what about that? I can certainly see how a person could take a *one-down* position around someone they felt was superior to them. But do you suppose we can recognize strengths others have while remaining horizontal?"

Judy nodded. "Sure. I don't think you have to denigrate yourself just because someone else is better at something. After all, no one can have *all* the strengths. Not even Frank Savage."

"Yes, and I certainly didn't get the sense that he was shrinking from my presence!" Dot chuckled. "He was still Frank. But it was maybe the first time I didn't feel like he was looking down at me or trying to control me. I felt like a colleague. If I hadn't, I'm sure I never would have returned to Bellweather.

"With all that in mind, I invite you all to look around the room. Do your relationships here feel *horizontal* to you? And did they feel that way when we began yesterday?"

Zane looked around again. What he noticed immediately was how different he felt now about Rita and Cree, and Dot and Ricardo. He was of course Rita's and Cree's superior at work, but he felt like he could hear them now, whereas before he wouldn't have been interested. Dot and Ricardo were different. Although he wouldn't have been able to articulate it before, he had previously shrunk himself before them, although for different reasons—Ricardo for his superior intellect, and Dot because whatever he did, people still liked and revered her more. He still recognized these strengths in them, but he didn't feel intimidated by them. Not as much anyway.

"Things certainly feel more horizontal to me now," Zane volunteered.

"That's what happens when you begin to offer your *du*," Dot replied.

"To review, then," she continued, "the first element of offering your *du* is to allow space between yourself and others, and the second is that there is no status differential in *du*. Some of us might have higher or lower status in terms of our position in our organizations, but that carries no meaning to us in moments of *I-You* relation. There is no higher or lower there. Only *du*.

"Now, to introduce a third element of the *du*, let me tell you another story.

"I was in Las Vegas a few years ago and went to a magic show. I was completely mesmerized by what the magician was doing. I knew it was all illusion, of course, but I couldn't for the life of me figure any of it out. I was transfixed with interest and kept being utterly surprised by what was happening. I was like a young child, eyes wide open, taking in a new and beautiful world for the first time. To say that I was *watching* or *seeing* the show doesn't at all capture what was going on. I was rather *beholding* it. To *behold* something is to be filled with wonder and open to surprise.

"Which brings us to the third aspect of offering one's *du*. When offering others our *du*, we don't try to see them in a particular way or as a particular something or someone, whether positive or negative. We are not managing how we see. We are not looking at others through concepts that sort the world for us into neat little buckets. Rather, we are *beholding* others, as if for the first time.

"To *behold* is to be wide open to wonder and surprise. It's a word that reminds us to encounter others without concepts or preconceived ideas. Each person is a one-of-a-kind marvel, a magic act of their own, and *beholding* is an idea that can remind us of this. With that in mind, I have a question for you. While we've been together these two days, have you been *beholding* others or merely seeing them?"

Zane thought back over their time together—Eliza playing Ricardo in tic-tac-toe, she and Sam going at each other but also having productive

OFFERING YOUR *DU*

dialogue, Pam's many interesting observations, Cree being a tree hugger, Stuart suddenly surfacing after total silence, his dad's surprising apology to Dot. Each of these was completely unexpected. It seemed to him like he had been *beholding*, at least in those moments.

But what about the rest of the time? the voice within him asked. *Have you really been beholding, or have you been locked up in your head?*

His thoughts turned to Laney. When was the last time he had encountered her anew and truly *beheld* her rather than merely *seen* her? He wasn't sure. *How about the kids?* he asked himself. When they were little, every moment was a beholding. *But now?* The fact that he talked with them only sporadically, and even then mostly about nothing, showed a profound lack of curiosity about them and their lives. He shook his head. *How long have I been locked up in this room, thinking that that was living?*

"So," Dot continued, "we've talked about three elements of the *du*— space or *difference*, *horizontalness*, and *beholding*.

"The fourth element of offering our *du* is something we've already discussed: It is that we allow ourselves to be affected, moved, and changed by the other. In *I-It* interactions, we keep control, including control over our own willingness to feel. In *I-You* relations, by contrast, we lay down the barrier that is keeping others from touching us."

This comment penetrated Zane because he realized that in some ways he *had* begun to lay down that barrier. He could tell because he was thinking and feeling things he'd never before considered or experienced.

"Here are the four elements we've discussed around offering our *du*—*allow space and difference*; *engage horizontally*; *don't just see, behold*; and *be open to being changed.*

OFFERING YOUR *DU*

- Allow space and difference.
- Engage horizontally.
- Don't just see, *behold.*
- Be open to being changed.

186 **YOU AND WE**

"With these ideas top of mind," Dot said, "we're going to take a break. It's now 1 PM, so we've been going for quite a while! We have some sack lunches waiting for you in the hallway. Let's take an hour for lunch. I invite you to take this time to be like Cree and to go out and enjoy the nature of this place up close and intimately. Feel free to wander the grounds wherever you would like. *Behold* what's around you. See the wonder. Take some time alone if you'd like or spend the time with each other. Try to let what we've been exploring together settle in a bit. If you spend time together, offer your *du*. And then come back with your very best questions.

"We'll start up again at 2 PM.

"Have a great lunch!"

PART IV

THE RELATIONAL LEAP

22

Alone

Rita, Judy, and Cree approached Zane about spending their break time together. He knew that would be a good idea but couldn't handle the thought of it at that moment. He needed to get away, to get outside, to clear his mind, to breathe. He said he might be able to meet toward the end of the hour and left the room in haste.

He knew where he wanted to go.

About a quarter mile northeast of the museum's main building, atop a knoll that was the highest place on the grounds, stood a massive green head that looked like a cross between a dinosaur and something Zane couldn't place.[43] Pegs sticking out of the figure where the ears should be gave it a Frankensteinian air.

He had seen the sculpture or figure or whatever it was the day before from the helicopter. It was at once playful and menacing, comforting and disconcerting. Most importantly of all, it was *away*.

He figured that most of his classmates would be heading into the trees that spread to the south and east from the building. But Zane just wanted to go up. Up and away. To the dinosaur. And he had no idea why.

190   YOU AND WE

He passed the place where their helicopter had landed the day before, which was at the base of the hill from where the giant figure lorded over the grounds. From there, he could cut directly up the slope, walking through the grasses and wildflowers that graced the hill, or take the longer route on the path. He elected to take the path, which circled him up and around the far side of the hill.

Zane wanted to process everything that was going through his head, but he instinctively pushed it away for the moment. He needed space from his internal arguments, and the green giant on the hill was the very thing to keep his attention diverted.

As he got closer, he noticed that the figure was actually two halves of different heads fitted oddly together. From the south, he had thought it was a dinosaur, but as he now approached from the north, the head on that side looked more like a pony. Flowers were beginning to bloom out of the two halves, making it a kind of prehistoric Chia Pet. It stood about 40 feet tall, with a distinct gap between the two sides.

Hmm, space between them, he thought. *That's an interesting illustration of what we've been discussing. I wonder what the artist was thinking.*

Zane took the sandwich out of his sack lunch and ate while he thought. He slowly circled the figure over and over, peering into the space between the halves and studying the figures and their effect. Their shapes looked somehow familiar, resembling childhood toys he might have played with. *Or was it the dinosaur from* Toy Story? he wondered. *What was his name? Rex, I believe. Okay, you'll be Rex, then.*

"You're as alive as the trees are, Rex," he said aloud to the figure, "what with all the flowers that are blooming as your skin. And if Cree can have conversations with the trees, then I can certainly talk with you. I just need someone to listen.

"So, where to begin?"

Zane started by telling Rex about Laney—about how they met, what made him fall in love, and their happy early years. Then he told Rex about the kids. How he thought Jackson was dead when he was born, and how Allison couldn't get to sleep unless he held her in his arms and sang to her while they danced. Most nights, he crooned her to sleep with Sinatra.

His favorite of Sinatra's songs was "My Way." It was the song of a man feeling he had lived a life that was full, and that he had done it in his own way. It was a triumphant song, and Zane used to hold Allison in his arms, dancing her all around the room, feeling full along with Sinatra, and looking forward to living a life for which Sinatra's crescendo-ing score could be his anthem. And yet, here he was, recounting that life, alone, to a massive metal dinosaur.

Zane sat down on the bench that faced the figure's face and started to weep.

Another song came to his mind, slowly fading in like background music to his tears. This one, too, was connected to a core memory. A week or so before Laney left, he walked into their home after work and was greeted by a melancholy yet soulful song by Gladys Knight. Laney was in her office while the song filled the air of their home. It was a number Zane had always loved, as it had been popular in the Nashville clubs during his wilder days. The memory washed over him again, and he began to sing softly and haltingly to Rex.

The verses told the story of a couple whose love and relationship were long gone but who couldn't work up the courage to say goodbye. Miserable together over many years, and yet afraid of being alone, they kept hanging on, each of them faking and pretending. They knew it was over, but neither one of them wanted to be the first to say it. As the song built, and as all the lies they had told themselves to keep the charade going were perhaps for the first time spoken and acknowledged, they finally arrived at the word they had been avoiding. And this time, instead of turning away, one of them finally had the courage to say it: *Goodbye*.

As Zane sang, it began to dawn on him that this song hadn't *just happened* to be playing when he walked into the house that evening.

The lyrics articulated the sad story and state of their marriage, and, with Gladys Knight as her voice, Laney was telling Zane that they were over.

The song was her farewell letter! She was telling me goodbye! With that realization, he started bawling. *She's really gone!* A wave of memories washed over him: that first and only swim class, Laney swaying in the Nashville clubs as he sang, their wedding, the births of their children, their disagreements, their arguments, and ultimately their silence. He hung his head and stared at the now tearstained ground at his feet. "Farewell to you, too, my love," he said aloud, choking out the words. "Goodbye."

He sat in silence for about 10 minutes. A gentle wind from the southwest made the grasses on the slope bend and wave in his direction. The trees to the south of him swayed merrily in the breeze. And the shudders that had rolled through his body along with his sobs slowly worked their way through his system.

He looked back up at Rex. "Thank you, sir. Thank you for listening. You've been a kind friend."

He looked at his watch. He'd been gone for 35 minutes. They would be starting up again in 25. He stood up and grabbed the bag that held his half-eaten lunch. *I'd better start heading back.*

He took the other way back—walking away from Rex on the gravel path that led eastward before bending to the south along the eastern edge of the tree line.

As he walked, he noticed someone else walking toward him. It was the professorial figure of Ricardo Bloom.

Ricardo waved to Zane as he approached.

"I've been looking for you, Zane," he said. "I'm so glad I found you!"

"What do you need?" Zane asked.

"I owe you an apology."

23

Wholes or Parts

Do you remember that meeting we had in Cambridge two years ago?" Ricardo asked Zane as they walked.

"Of course. That's the day you turned down the best opportunity of your lifetime."

"Possibly." Ricardo smiled. "But whether I made the right decision or not, I showed up in a poor way, and for that, I am truly sorry."

"It didn't seem like you were really listening to me."

"Oh, I was. Until I wasn't," Ricardo replied.

"Why?" Zane asked. "I couldn't figure out why you weren't at all interested. I was prepared to give you equity in the company, for heaven's sake! But you didn't seem to care."

"I couldn't get past something."

"What?"

Ricardo stopped walking. "Look, I don't want to upset you, Zane, but I feel like I owe you an explanation. What I couldn't get past was that you kept talking about yourself—about you and your father. I knew something of what Dot had done over the years at Bellweather, but you never even mentioned her. In fact, when I brought her up, you changed the subject, and that struck me as strange. And worrisome.

"In the scientific community, we are careful to give credit to everyone who has gone before. We realize that doing so doesn't diminish oneself in the least but rather establishes one as a credible, trustworthy colleague. We cite like crazy. We don't take credit for other people's discoveries and contributions, and we give people their due. So, I wasn't comfortable with what was going on at Bellweather and didn't want to be a part of it. It felt like a collective that was overlooking or burying the contributions of its members, which was too unscientific a practice to condone as a scientist."

Normally, a thousand ideas would have swept through Zane's mind—countless lines of defense and attack. He would have modulated his response to make the most desirable impression. He would have changed his voice as needed, his expression, his manner. If he'd had the time, he would have practiced. But all that was gone. He was empty.

"But what if you're trying to build a team?" he asked weakly. "Isn't it better to keep everyone focused on the whole rather than on individuals? Isn't that what we're learning here?"

"Quite the opposite, actually," Ricardo answered. "Remember Seurat's painting from yesterday? We've been focusing on relation, which is about how different things coming together, like the points in Seurat's painting, give birth to something beyond any one of them. The whole is the offspring of the parts in relation. Putting it in the terms of our water metaphor, you get water only if you value what hydrogen and oxygen bring. Water has no water-making force of its own. Hydrogen and oxygen are what make it happen. If you forget that, the water will dry up. Likewise, individuals in relation are the lifeblood of every effort, and if you forget them, or erase them, you weaken the bonds that make the whole even possible."

"Hmm," Zane said. "I guess I've been off about that too."

"One more thing. Forcing a focus on a collective whole without a deep appreciation and celebration of the contributions that make it possible is a totalitarian way of leading. Any effort that demands allegiance to an abstracted *We* that minimizes its members is an oppressive force, usually led by a leader who is more concerned about themselves, or about something else they value, than the people who make it all possible. Leaders who promote the whole at the expense of each other are usually implicitly promoting themselves, as they are the only natural faces of the collective. *Whole*-promotion is usually *leader*-promotion in disguise."

"That's what you thought when we met?" Zane asked. "That I was erasing Dot and promoting myself?"

"Not necessarily yourself, but, at the very least, something you yourself hold dear. Rightly or wrongly, that's what I thought, Zane. And I should have raised it with you, for two reasons. First, telling you would have given you the chance to set me straight if I was wrong. And second, if I was correct, sharing my concerns might have helped you. As it was, however, I wasn't prepared to be your partner, even in that conversation. I wasn't willing to give you my *du*. However, over the last two days, as I've reflected on our conversations, it has struck me how I violated everything we have been discussing. That's why I want to apologize to you. I'm sorry that I locked myself away when we met."

"Can I ask you something?" Zane said.

"Yes, anything."

"Would you be interested in joining us now if I asked?"

"I'd be willing to talk about it, but you need to know that the concerns I had then, if valid, are concerns I still carry."

"I understand."

They walked in silence for another 20 seconds or so.

"*Are* they still valid?" Ricardo asked.

Zane didn't answer right away. He was battling within himself over what and how much to say.

"You don't need to manage this conversation," Ricardo said. "You can just say it."

A war was raging within Zane. The quieter voice within him was now equal and gaining in volume over the narrative he had been telling himself—the story of why *responsibility* required him to force Dot out, that she had stolen the spotlight that his father deserved, and that the company was now much better off under his own leadership. The once quieter voice countered: *But the company isn't better off, and you know it. Our top-line numbers have been flat while our bottom line is in free fall due to our huge capital expenditures. And it's not the same place anymore culturally. Don't blame what you did on something outside of you—on some amorphous idea like* Responsibility *requiring you to do it. That's just another concept inside your head. You did what you did because that's what you wanted to do. Everything else is just a story.*

They came to a large black art piece that looked like a massive, many-legged sand crab or spider composed of repeating geometrical cells.[44] It crouched powerfully on a bed of gravel. Like Rex to the north, it was both menacing and inviting. They turned to the right on the path directly in front of the sculpture, bending their way toward the museum.

Zane slowed and stopped. He turned to face Ricardo. "It's true that I forced Dot out. And it's also true that I've been trying to rid the company of its fixation on her. So, if that's what you're concerned with, then I think your concerns are still valid.

"But I would just add that I think both of those have been the right moves for the company."

"Why?" Ricardo asked.

"Why do I think they've been the right moves?" Zane repeated.

"Yes."

"Because I think that Dot, for all the good she did for us—and she did a *ton*, I don't want to minimize that—undermined my father's legacy."

"How?"

"She garnered too much attention herself, both internally within the company and externally. I think she enjoyed becoming the face of Bellweather, and I think we're better off not having a face."

"Just a *name* instead," Ricardo said.

Zane looked at him. "Yes, *Bellweather*."

"Not *Savage*?" Ricardo asked.

Zane didn't respond immediately.

"Can I ask you something?" Ricardo said.

"Sure."

"The story you're telling me sounds an awful lot like the story your father was telling himself when *he* forced Dot out. But it seems he ended up thinking that was a mistake. Do you think it might be possible that you're mistaken too?"

Two memories rushed into Zane's mind. The first was of the day his father announced Dot as CEO. The event was held outside on the quad between foundations of buildings that were just beginning to rise in Pittsburgh. Although his father had been at the head of the company for decades at that point, his relationship with the workforce had been mixed, to say the least. He tended to micromanage, and he didn't suffer fools—two personality traits that lived with him even after Dot had returned to the company. People mostly feared him. Zane had spent the first 20 years of his life fearing him as well, so he completely understood the feeling. Still, this was his *father*—the founder of the company, the person without whom there would be no Bellweather. He deserved respect.

So, Zane remembered feeling a twinge of anger at the excitement pulsating through the crowd that day—a palpable happiness that Frank Savage was going to hand the reins of the company over to Dot Kessler. Zane didn't have anything against Dot at the time. He liked her as much as anyone else. But the level of enthusiasm for the change felt to him like a slap in his father's face.

The second memory was more visceral. It was from his father's funeral. Zane gave the eulogy. Frank Savage had lived an amazing life. He was a veteran of the Vietnam War, receiving the Purple Heart for an injury to his leg that caused him to limp the rest of his life, an injury he sustained while trying to carry one of his injured men to safety. He received his PhD from Penn State and had started Bellweather in his backyard while still a student, along with his good friend Earl Crandin, who was killed in a car accident five year later. Frank built the company in those early years largely through his own grit and determination and bankrolled it with his own savings.

All this effort and success was the continuation of a family story that went back centuries. Frank Savage was a direct descendent of one of the earliest settlers from England, Thomas Savage, who was a 13-year-old ship hand on the vessel that led the establishment of the first permanent settlement in the New World at Jamestown, Virginia. Thomas Savage played a prominent role in those early decades in the New World and is said to be the source of the longest continuing family name in America: *Savage*. Frank Savage had fierce pride in his family name and history, and he passed that pride on to his children. *Savage* was not just a name to them; it was a trailblazing heritage.

What came to Zane's mind again at that moment was that Dot didn't attend the funeral. After all Frank Savage had done for her, she couldn't make it. The almost overwhelming number of flowers she arranged to have delivered for the funeral was no substitute for not being there herself, and her absence confirmed the suspicion that had been building within Zane, that Dot didn't respect his father. The heritage that was so important to everything that happened in the family, including the building of Bellweather, was not hers. She had no personal investment in it. As such, she couldn't really be trusted to do right by that heritage.

Ricardo's question still hung in the air: *Do you think it might be possible that you're mistaken too?*

"No, Ricardo, I don't think I'm mistaken. It isn't jealousy in my case, like it evidently was for my father. It's about responsibility and honor."

"*Whose* honor, and *whose* responsibility?" Ricardo asked.

"*Honor* for my father. This company is his legacy, and I'm *responsible* now for that legacy."

"So, I was right, then," Ricardo said.

"About what?"

"About my suspicions when we met. You were—and still are, it seems—primarily concerned with yourself."

"Not at all! Being concerned about my father's legacy is not a concern for myself."

"Oh really, Zane *Savage*?

"And by the way, not that it's likely to make a difference, but I feel like I have gotten to know your father over the last year—quite deeply, in fact. And do you know why? Because he's about the only person Dot ever speaks of. She lost her own father too. And when she talks about them, I can tell that she loved your dad every bit as much as her own."

"Wait, she lost her father? I didn't know that."

"Yes. It was a freak boating accident. In Seattle, I believe."

Zane shook his head.

So, she lost her dad too. All the more reason she should have known to be at my father's funeral, he said to himself. *Maybe she wanted to be there, but something got in the way*, came his other voice. *Hell, you didn't even know her father died! You didn't make his funeral either.*

"I have two more thoughts for you before we get back to the group, Zane. The first is that I think your team is wanting to meet with you."

"Yes, when we broke for lunch, we talked about getting together. I'm hoping to catch them before we start up again."

"That's great. So let me say this: Do you remember what I said about the totalitarian leader—the one who demands allegiance to the whole without real appreciation for the parts that make it all possible?"

Zane nodded. "Yes."

"I think that's you, Zane."

Zane stopped again. "That's not true, Ricardo. Not even close. My whole focus is on *seeing the humanity in people*."

"Which, again, although a really positive idea, is in your own head. Real people are over there," he said, pointing to the museum. "And they're messy, imperfect, odd, sometimes infuriating, and at other times completely brilliant. But you'll never find real people in that nice, tidy concept you've built for yourself in your mind. You have to get out and join them.

"But here's the problem: If your real concern is the Bellweather or Savage legacy rather than the people who are making their own time investments to create that legacy along with you, then you'll *never* join them. And if you don't bring your own difference to the encounter, and value the differences and contributions that they themselves bring, you won't make water either, and the legacy you're dreaming of won't turn out quite the way you want. So, I would just say that if you want to have a productive meeting with your colleagues, something in the next two minutes is going to need to break through the pride you are carrying that is making them second-class citizens in your company rather than first-class citizens in their own. And I'm wondering what that something will be."

Zane didn't say anything for a few moments. Then he whispered, "I didn't know that her father died." He thought of how his own family was coming apart. "It's so hard to lose your family."

Ricardo nodded but didn't say anything.

Zane stopped again. "You know what really bothers me about Dot, though?"

"What?"

"That she seems so perfect. All I've heard for years from my dad, my mom, and all the people at work is how great Dot is. I'm so tired of it."

Ricardo chuckled.

"Why are you laughing?"

"Because just last night she was telling me what a mess she thinks she is. She feels like she's failing at everything that matters most, and that she's not up to the challenges she's facing."

"What? Dot? Really?"

"Come on, Zane, she's messy like the rest of us. Well, maybe not as messed up as you are." He laughed. "But as messy as the rest of us."

Zane chuckled painfully. "You don't know the half of it, believe me."

"Then you put on quite an act, Zane. I think you'd be better off if you lost the act.

"Oh, and if you want to ask Dot about her problems, she's right over there," he said, pointing toward the entrance of the museum.

24

Another Chance

As Zane approached Dot, she looked up and smiled at him. "Hey, Zane," she said. "How are you feeling about everything?"

"I'm still processing. It's a lot to take in."

"Yes, it is," she agreed. "I'm really glad you're here, though. It's been good to see you again. I see a lot of your dad in you. And that's a big compliment."

Zane smiled and looked into her eyes. For the first time, he registered the warmth in them. "Ricardo mentioned that your father passed away too," he said after a moment of silence.

"Yes, almost the same time yours did in fact. Sailing accident that put him into a coma. I had to rush to Seattle when that happened, which is the reason I missed your dad's funeral, by the way. As it was, my father never woke up, and I missed saying goodbye to the two men that have meant more to me that anyone in my life—my dad and yours. Life really sucks sometimes, you know?"

Zane teared up and nodded. "Yeah, it does. It really does." He lifted his head and met Dot's eyes again. *Why do they look different now?* "No one knows it yet," he said, "but Laney and I are getting divorced." Like his comment the day before about *breaking*, he hadn't intended to say it; it just came out.

"Oh, I'm so sorry, Zane. That breaks my heart. I'm so sorry."

Zane stood there looking at the ground and nodding, fighting back the tears. He could feel the anguish rising through his chest and into his throat. "Yeah, anyway, it won't be long now. She's staying in Georgetown, and I'm in our place in Alexandria. Like you say, life really sucks sometimes."

"Is there anything I can do for you?"

"Maybe call her? See how she's doing? You always meant a lot to her."

"I'll do that, Zane. By the way, I've been through a divorce too. So, I know the pain."

"I didn't even know you were married."

"Years ago," she answered.

"I don't remember you having any kids."

"No, we divorced before we had children. That probably made it a lot easier. How are your kids doing—how are Jackson and Allison?"

"They don't know yet."

"Oh, yeah, then that's tough. I'm so sorry."

"No one knows yet," Zane said. "I'm too embarrassed to tell anyone."

"Except me. I'm honored that you would, Zane. That's saying something."

"Yeah, and I honestly don't know why." He chuckled sadly. "Not having much of a relationship anymore maybe made it easier."

"Even so, I'm honored. And you don't have to worry, I won't tell anyone. That's all up to you and your timing. But I *will* reach out to Laney as you said, just to see how she's doing."

"That would be good."

"I wish we could keep talking, Zane," she said. "There's so much to catch up on. But we have the others to get back to."

"Do you mind if I ask you something before we head in?"

"Of course not."

ANOTHER CHANCE

"Do you really think we're off track at Bellweather?"

She sighed. "Yes, I do. I'm really worried about you guys. The need for your technology is so great that I'm worried the demand that's about to come your way is going to completely crush the company. I don't think your foundations are strong enough to withstand what's coming. I'm worried you're going to crumble under the weight."

"Will it make you happy at all if we do? Would you feel vindicated by that?"

"Ahh, Zane. Look, I was really hurt how everything went down. And if I'm honest, there were days when hearing about problems at Bellweather did bring me some solace. But I think I'm mostly past that."

"Mostly?"

Dot thought about it. "Yeah, mostly. I have this weird need to feel wanted." She laughed softly. "I think it probably developed sometime during my childhood. And that immature part of me is still there. I've been working on it, but being forced out of Bellweather after all those years was, shall we say, a *challenge* for that part of me. But hey, here we are again. And it's not so bad, is it?"

Zane laughed. "No, it's not so bad. What's next after this?" he asked. "Is this just a two-day program and we all go our own ways, or is there more to it?"

"Which would you prefer?" She smiled at him.

"I think we'd all benefit from more time together, and from helping each other with our challenges. The challenges we're facing won't get fixed in two days."

"I'll tell you what—we'll talk about what's next in the group, okay?" Zane nodded.

"Shall we go in, then?"

Zane looked at the words on the lobby wall again as he passed:

Substance so stirred at its depth
To result in a change in essence
Opening a path for transformation

From solitariness

To synthesis

It was starting to make sense.

On their way back to the room, Zane saw Rita, Judy, and Cree deep in conversation down the hall. "All the groups are really working on things," Dot said, "so we're going to extend the break by another 30 minutes. Take your time with your team, Zane. Apply what you've learned. Oh, and remember to offer your *du*." She winked at him.

He thanked her and approached his colleagues. *Offer my* du*, offer my* du, he repeated to himself, trying to remember the details. *What were those four things again?* He replayed the conversation in his head. *Honor the space and difference between us; engage horizontally; don't just see but get out of your head and behold; and*—he racked his brain for the last one—*oh yeah, be open to being changed.*

"Sorry, guys, I meant to be back sooner," he said, greeting them. "Dot said we have some extra time, thankfully. What have you been tackling? How can I help?"

Rita and Judy glanced at each other and then back at Zane.

"What would you like to tackle, Boss?"

"No, no, no, you've already been working on things. Let's keep going on whatever that is. Bring me up to speed if you'd like and then let's keep moving forward."

Rita and Judy glanced at each other again. Cree stood, just looking at him.

"Okay, guys, what is it?" Zane asked. "I can tell when I'm the awkward one at the party."

"Honestly, we don't have an agenda we're working on," Judy said. "We figured that we needed to get to know each other better before we could productively tackle anything. After all, our *depth of knowing others* score on the assessment was abysmal. And we realized we were all part of that. So, we've mostly been learning about each other. It's been really good. I'm sorry you've missed it."

ANOTHER CHANCE

"How do I catch up?"

"By slowing down, Boss," Rita said. "This can't be a one-off thing that we just hurry through."

Zane nodded. "Understood. Then what do we do now?"

"How about if we learn about *you*?" Cree said. "I don't think I really know you. I know the *persona* of Zane Savage, but not the person."

"Okay," Zane said, "we can do that. What would you like to know?"

"No, that's not how we've been doing it," Rita said.

Zane was starting to feel annoyed at her again. But then he remembered that to offer his *du*, he needed to approach the interaction horizontally. He could feel himself tipping away from that.

"What do you mean, Rita?"

"We're not just sets of facts—where we were born, where we went to school, our families, and so on. That's just surface stuff. We want to know each other beyond that. Deeper than that. We want to know what makes us each tick, what we care about, the challenges we are facing, how we think about different things, why we react the ways we do. And we want to let all that work on us. So, let's do this: I'll throw out a topic, and then let's all talk and question each other about it. Fair enough?"

Zane shrugged his shoulders. "Okay."

"All right, then," she continued, "here's the topic: What has made you most uncomfortable over these two days?"

"You mean besides this conversation we're having right now?" Zane joked.

Rita smiled. "It could be this conversation if you'd like. What makes you uncomfortable with it?"

Space. Horizontal. Behold. Openness to change, Zane repeated to himself, like a drill sergeant leading his conscripts in the art of offering their *du*. But then his other voice challenged him: *Don't make those, too, into concepts! That will just keep you in your head. Let them invite you out of your head. You don't have to work hard here, Zane. Relation isn't built; it's already there. Just drop out of the story you're always telling yourself and others. Forget the seeming. Leave the room behind. Behold them and engage.*

"What's been most uncomfortable has been seeing Dot again."

"Why?" Rita asked.

"Well, that's an interesting question. I thought it was because of how things went down between us. We didn't end on good terms."

"Who said you ended?" Cree commented.

Zane chuckled. "I guess you're right. We didn't end after all."

"Nothing really does," Cree said.

"So, then, why do you *now* think you've been uncomfortable being with her again?" Rita followed up.

Dot's story about the conversation with his father flashed into his mind. "I don't know. I keep thinking of my dad, unable to offer an apology. I'm wondering if that's me too."

"Yeah, I get that," Cree said. "It's always darkest right before the dawn."

Zane looked at him, a puzzled look on his face. "You are an interesting person, Cree. It's like you're Henry David Thoreau's engineering twin or something."

"Haven't read him, but he's on my list. So, about that darkness . . ."

Zane shifted his feet uncomfortably. "Yeah, I don't know. There might be something there, but I can't see it."

"I can," Rita said.

Zane looked at her. "What do you mean?"

"Nothing's only inside," she replied. "That's one of the things I'm taking away from this. I can't see what's inside you, Zane, but I see what's happening on the outside, and I can feel the relational impact."

"So, what are you seeing?"

"That's not as important as what *you* are seeing."

"Well, what am I supposed to do with that?" Zane asked. "Help me out."

"Here, maybe I can help," Cree said. "Because this isn't just your problem, Zane—it's *our* problem. We're all involved in it. Isn't that part of what we're learning here—that everything is relational? It's so tempting to pin things on one person. But every *thesis* has its *antithesis*. Even if that antithesis is silence, like mine has been. Case in point: Do you remember in January when you came in and demanded that I fire Steve Bramwell?"

"Sure. He was a problem and needed to go."

"But that was a Band-Aid fix to a larger situation."

"The situation being *what*?"

"That we don't talk about problems we're seeing. For example, I never said anything to you about how I was feeling about the Steve situation. I thought we should take a different approach, but I didn't push back and say anything to you. I just held my tongue and did what I was told."

"But, Cree, I wouldn't have had to talk with you about it if you'd done the right thing in the first place."

Cree didn't say anything. He just let Zane's words hang in the air.

"That right there," Rita said.

Zane turned and looked at her.

"Don't you see, Boss? We can't give you feedback. It always has to be *your* way."

My Way. Sinatra's song came to Zane's mind again.

"It's not fair to put it on you, Zane," Cree said. "I'm the one who didn't say anything then—and *most* of the time, for that matter. That's on *me*."

"Yes, but if you didn't because you felt saying something would be futile," Zane said, "then that's on *me*."

"Steve wasn't a problem alone, and neither are you and me," Cree replied. "What Steve was doing was an expression of what the culture allowed. And me staying silent and you giving directives are part of that same culture. We're all part of it. And we're influencing the other parts. It's not so much that it's *on* either of us, but that we're both *in* it."

"But if everyone is responsible, then no one is," Zane countered.

"Said Descartes, probably." Cree smiled.

Zane looked at him quizzically.

"If we're all just separate, like Descartes believed," Cree explained, "then of course some*one* is responsible. But that leads away from a relational view. Something that Dot or Ricardo said yesterday got me thinking how, from a relational point of view, it's more accurate and helpful to think in terms of *influence* or *impact* rather than *responsibility*, as all of us usually have some level of impact on an issue. Instead of assigning blame, a leader taking a relational approach might consider questions like these: *How am I part of this problem? How have I helped to invite it? How might others have done the same? How have we done this together, in response to each other?*

"When things go wrong," he continued, "it's tempting to look for who's responsible. But I think the truth is that invitation and influence go in every direction. We are both cause and effect, actor and acted upon, influencer and the influenced. We're way more involved in what's happening around and within us than we normally think. The size of another's responsibility in our eyes should never blind us to our own influence and responsibility, whatever that might be. Anyway, that's the way it seems to me."

Zane looked at Cree in wonder. "Who *are* you? Seriously."

Cree shrugged. "I'm nobody. Just a guy trying to figure things out."

Zane shook his head. "Honestly, I haven't known you at all, Cree. That's on me."

"No," Cree said with a chuckle. "I'm in that too."

"You know, it occurs to me," Judy said, "that as a way to combat the impulse to assign blame to individuals alone, we could institute a practice like an *influence audit*, for example, where we tackle issues together and try to assess our own impact on them by finding the strands of our own influence."

Zane nodded. "I like that."

"You do?" Rita asked.

"Yes, absolutely."

"Then why don't we do one now?" she said. "I propose that we examine our *Lead Like a Savage* program and our impact on it."

ANOTHER CHANCE 209

Zane bristled. "You know that's not its name."

"Yes, but I think we should consider why people call it that. When *you're* not in earshot, anyway."

"Oh, I've heard it. So, what are you thinking about it?"

"I have thoughts, for sure. But I think we should start by thinking about how people are responding to it and what its impact is in the company."

"Okay, and what do you think?" Zane asked.

"I think people are weaponizing it against each other," Rita replied. "And from what we've learned here, I think that's because the program concentrates on what's inside people. While it might be helpful to concentrate on what's inside *ourselves*, when we start accusing others with that same analysis, things go off the rails. I say that because I've been feeling it in me. I look around at other people and accuse them either verbally or in my head of not seeing others the way we're trying to train people to see others. And I do that most, to be honest, Boss, toward *you*. Yesterday you said that you had been *breaking* toward Dot. But I now realize that I've been *breaking* toward you in the same kind of way."

Judgments he had been making about Rita ran through Zane's mind—*unreasonable, out for herself, not a team player, cantankerous, troublemaker, rabble-rouser*. His mind stopped at the last one. *The people in the company who have resisted me are rabble that she is rousing? Really?* He considered what that glimpse into his psyche implied about whether he had been allowing space for difference from his own ideas or agenda. *With no space, there is no relation*, he remembered. Ricardo's searing words echoed in his mind: *If you want to have a productive meeting with your colleagues, something is going to need to break through the pride you are carrying that is making them second-class citizens in your company rather than first-class citizens in their own. And I'm wondering what that something will be.* Zane looked at Rita and was shocked to discover that that something would be *her*.

Zane let out a long exhale. "I do the same thing, Rita. And I'm sorry to say that I've been doing it toward you too. No wonder we've both been experiencing our relationship at a -2 level."

"Which I've been blaming on you, by the way!" Rita said. "*Sure, our relationship is at -2, but that's on him!* That's what I've been thinking."

"Me too!" Zane laughed. "Which means I've been looking at relation in a nonrelational way!" He shook his head in wonder. "I'm really sorry about that, Rita. And I see now, when I'm doing that, that I'm totally in my own head, keeping myself divided from you. And, by the way, calling me *Boss* makes me wonder how I've been inviting 'Boss' talk up until now too. Obviously, you don't feel like I've offered you my *du*."

"I suppose not," she replied.

"You can call me *du*," he said.

"It's not just a matter of words," Rita responded. "It's those things that Dot shared with us. But you're not the only one of us who needs to work on them. I'd like you to feel that I'm offering my *du* too."

"Fair enough. There's plenty of room to grow from -2."

"There sure is," she agreed.

"So, what do you think we need to do with the program, Rita?" he asked.

"If I had to list the problems with it," she responded, "I'd say they would sort into four categories. First of all, it's *individualistic* rather than *relational*. Secondly, because of that misunderstanding, what it teaches individuals to do isn't quite right. Thirdly, it's heavily weighted toward just one or two of the relational quadrants. Finally, and this is probably the biggest issue from my point of view, the program feels like it's being done *to* people rather than *with* people, engaging everyone's thoughts and perspectives. I think it needs to be completely revamped."

"So, you're saying you like it, then," Zane deadpanned.

She laughed. "It's the best," she said sarcastically.

"Well, so what do we do? Honestly, I'm a bit overwhelmed with the idea of redoing it all."

"This isn't just on you, Zane," Judy said. "You have a team here. And we can get Dot's help too.

"If you want it."

25

Together Differently

Welcome back, everyone," Dot said. "How did you enjoy your lunch break and your time together?"

"Fantastic," Jorn said.

"Why *fantastic*, Jorn?"

"Because, as a team, we had the best discussion we've ever had about some of the issues that are dividing us. And I have to thank Stuart for standing strong with some unpopular viewpoints. And Pam for making sure we think through the various perspectives people in the company might have on these issues. We were trying to develop our *start-with-synthesis* muscle."

"That's great to hear, Jorn! Well done, PERC team. Anyone else?"

"This is the first time I've had real hope for my company in at least two years," Rita said.

"And why, Rita?"

"Because we just had the most real conversation and dialogue I've ever experienced in my professional life—right now, out in the hallway. We were straightforward with each other, honest, respectful, interested. That gives me a lot of hope. If we can hang onto it."

"That's terrific, Rita. I'm so happy to hear that! Huge kudos to the Bellweather team!

"I'm interested in hearing from the congressional team, too, but given what you from PERC and you from Bellweather have just shared, I'd first like you all to consider something. Think about how we were together when we began yesterday compared to how we're together now. How would you describe the difference?"

Everyone looked around at each other, smiling and acknowledging each other as their eyes met. "I'd say there's an openness that at least *I* didn't feel when we first started," Dexter shared.

"For me the word is *immediacy*," Cree said. "I was thinking about that over lunch, while meeting with my Bellweather colleagues. I didn't feel the barriers that my mind normally puts up between myself and others. It was like being out with the trees."

"Hmm, that's really beautiful, Cree. Thank you. If we were to redo our relational maps from yesterday, what do you think would happen to the scores?" Dot asked the group.

Zane thought about how he'd scored the relationships with Ricardo and Dot—at -1 and -2, respectively. *What would I score them at now?* He looked at each of them. *They'd at least be at 0. Maybe even at 1?*

"I'd score my relationships much higher," Sam said.

"Me too," Rita said.

"For sure, higher."

"Yes, higher."

"Way up."

"Can we redo the map?" Jorn asked. "I'd be curious."

"Do you all want to do that?" Dot asked.

Everyone around the room nodded enthusiastically. "Yes!"

"Okay, then I'll share a blank version of the chart with you. Go ahead and enter your scores and we'll see what we have."

Three minutes later, after importing everyone's scores, Dot broadcast both their old and new relational maps to the screen.

YESTERDAY

	ZANE	JUDY	RITA	CREE	ELIZA	SAM	DEXTER	ARLO	JORN	TIM	PAM	STUART	RICARDO	DOT	ave
ZANE (Bellweather -0.58)		0	-2	-1	0	0	0	1	0	0	0	0	-1	-2	-0.38
JUDY	0		0	-1	0	0	0	-1	0	0	0	0	1	2	0.08
RITA	-2	0		0	0	0	0	-1	0	0	0	0	0	2	-0.08
CREE	0	0	-1		0	-1	-1	0	0	0	1	0	0	0	-0.15
ELIZA (Congress -0.42)	-1	0	0	0		-2	-1	0	0	0	0	0	1	0	-0.23
SAM	0	0	0	0	-2		1	-1	0	0	0	0	1	1	0.00
DEXTER	0	0	0	0	0	1		0	0	0	0	0	0	2	0.23
ARLO	1	0	0	0	-1	-1	1		0	0	0	0	1	1	0.15
JORN (PERC -0.08)	0	0	0	0	0	-1	0	0		0	1	-1	0	0	-0.08
TIM	0	0	0	0	1	-1	-1	0	0		0	-1	0	0	-0.15
PAM	-1	0	1	1	0	1	1	0	0	1		0	1	1	0.46
STUART	0	0	0	1	1	0	0	1	-1	-1	1		0	0	0.15
RICARDO	-1	0	0	0	0	0	0	0	0	0	0	0		2	0.08
DOT	-2	2	1	0	1	1	2	0	0	1	0	0	2		0.62
ave	-0.46	0.15	-0.08	0.00	0.00	-0.23	0.15	-0.08	-0.08	0.08	0.23	-0.15	0.46	0.69	**0.05**

KEY: **-2** Division | **-1** Subtraction | **0** Addition | **1** Multiplication | **2** Compounding

TODAY

	ZANE	JUDY	RITA	CREE	ELIZA	SAM	DEXTER	ARLO	JORN	TIM	PAM	STUART	RICARDO	DOT	ave
ZANE (Bellweather 0.83)		1	0	1	2	1	1	2	1	0	2	0	1	1	1.00
JUDY	0		2	1	1	1	2	1	1	0	1	0	2	2	1.08
RITA	-1	1		1	1	0	1	0	0	0	2	0	0	2	0.54
CREE	1	2	1		1	0	0	0	1	0	2	1	1	2	0.92
ELIZA (Congress 0.92)	1	0	0	2		0	1	1	1	0	1	0	2	1	0.77
SAM	0	0	0	1	1		1	1	2	0	1	0	2	2	0.85
DEXTER	1	0	0	1	1	2		1	0	1	2	1	1	2	1.00
ARLO	1	1	1	1	1	0	1		1	0	1	1	1	2	0.92
JORN (PERC 1.08)	1	1	1	1	1	0	2	1		1	2	1	2	2	1.23
TIM	0	0	1	0	1	1	1	2	1		1	1	1	1	0.85
PAM	0	0	1	2	2	1	1	1	2	1		1	2	2	1.23
STUART	0	0	0	2	1	1	1	1	1	0	1		1	1	0.77
RICARDO	1	1	1	1	2	1	1	1	2	1	2	1		2	1.31
DOT	1	2	1	0	1	1	2	1	2	1	2	1	2		1.31
ave	0.46	0.69	0.69	1.08	1.23	0.69	1.15	1.00	1.15	0.38	1.54	0.62	1.38	1.69	**0.98**

KEY: **-2** Division | **-1** Subtraction | **0** Addition | **1** Multiplication | **2** Compounding

"Wow, that's a dramatic change!" Dexter said.

Zane studied the numbers. The Bellweather team number was up to 83 from -58. That was huge. He noticed that Rita still rated their work relationship in the negative. *But that's fair*, he reasoned. One good conversation doesn't erase a whole history. *We're still behind the other two groups, though.* Then he thought about his whole company. *I wonder how a full Bellweather cross-functional map would score.* He resolved to help his team build one in the coming weeks.

"So, if you look at the scores," Dot said, "you're rating our relationships significantly higher than yesterday. And I'm with you, Dex—it's a dramatic jump. Notice the increase in the overall average relationship score in the bottom right corner—98 now, compared to 05 yesterday. That's a jump from almost exactly *addition* on average to almost exactly *multiplication* on average. Do you realize how much money organizations around the world would pay to get that kind of a leap? If we were a team, our effectiveness together would be *way* better tomorrow than it was two days ago."

"*Can't* we be a team?" Jorn asked. "Is there a way we could stay connected through this process? I don't know about you all, but it has been tremendously helpful to learn about issues you are facing in your positions. It gives me a broader perspective from which to draw."

"Do the rest of you feel the same way?" Dot asked. "Would you like to stay connected, and maybe even continue to work on things together?"

"Yes," Zane said. "Very much."

"I'd like that," Eliza said. "I feel like I'm lagging way behind most of you, but I sometimes catch a glimmer of hope, at least for an instant, when I hear you processing things.

"And, if I can just add," she said, with a mischievous grin, "anything that can penetrate Zane Savage has power behind it."

Zane cracked up. "I'd pay to have Eliza Schuler make fun of me," he said.

"Oh, but you are, Zane, believe me. By the truckload. What's your tax bracket again?"

He laughed all the harder.

"I think we need to open this up to more people in Congress," Dexter said. "Four of us are a start, but we'll be trying to push a mighty big boulder up Everest if we go this alone."

"I agree with that," Arlo said. "But I also think that the example I shared earlier about the delegates at the Constitutional Convention points us in the right direction and might give us something to unite around. Consider the first line of the Constitution they penned: 'We the People of the United States,' they wrote, 'in order to form a more perfect Union . . .' Think about that phrase—*a more perfect Union*! The way they united in common cause, in the face of their differences, is what led, more than any other factor, to the successful creation of the country. *Their* more perfect union is what made the Constitution possible, and through that document they have called us to join with them in that same endeavor—to create a more perfect union between us. A unity not of sameness but of differences coming together. *E pluribus unum—out of many, one.* If that's not a summary of what we've been doing here over the last two days, I don't know what is.

"So, yes, Dexter, I second your motion to figure out how to involve more of our colleagues in this effort. And I also vote to figure out how to continue forward with this group. I've learned a lot from all of you."

"Have any of you on the Hill studied the era of our history that Mark Twain dubbed *the Gilded Age*?" Dot asked.

Eliza, Sam, Dexter, and Arlo looked at one another and shook their heads.

"It's a bit of history that might be relevant here," Dot said. "The Gilded Age ran roughly from 1870 to 1900. It was a time with uncanny resemblance to today in terms of the socioeconomic picture of the country and its polarized political climate. Society was becoming transformed by dramatic technological advances that, while improving conditions for people generally, were also generating massive increases in the wealth of the very few. Traditional industries were shuttering, corporate consolidations were pushing local proprietorships out of businesses, there was a great unease about whether the American experiment could survive, and the country was deeply polarized politically. Sound familiar?"

Everyone nodded.

"What's most interesting about that history is how the country reversed course, with lessons that show what is possible today. For any who are interested, I can recommend a couple of books that will get you into the remarkable parallels with our time and also detail how the country completely turned it around, socioeconomically and politically."[45]

"I don't know how much we can do from inside the system to turn it around," Eliza said. "Clearly, the current system rewards us for acting exactly as we are. Pressure for these changes needs to be exerted from the outside as well as the inside."

"That's precisely what happened coming out of the Gilded Age," Dot said. "Known as the *Progressive Era*—not *progressive* in terms of being on the *left* of the political spectrum, but progressive in terms of moving the country forward—insiders and outsiders worked to dramatically change the country's political system in ways that incentivized and rewarded politicians for working together more constructively, which paved the way for all the societal advances that followed.

"I share this with you for two reasons. First, I want to give you some optimism. We did it before; we can do it again. And secondly, given that Eliza just said that the system needs pressure from the outside, my question for you is, do you want to be part of that pressure? If you all want to keep meeting and working together, we can add political reform to the list of items we will be tackling, if you'd like. We can join the ranks of the reformers.

"We have frameworks and tools we can bring to bear in those discussions. Consider, for example, a four-quadrant analysis.

FOUR QUADRANT ANALYSIS

Outer

1 BEHAVIOR		**3 STRUCTURE**

Individual

That hinders | That helps

Changes

That hinders | That helps

Changes

2 ATTITUDE | **4 COMMUNITY**

That hinders | That helps

Changes

That hinders | That helps

Changes

Group

Inner

"We could consider various aspects of our political system through this four-dimensional lens—elections, campaign finance, House and Senate rules, legislation, and so on. Regarding each, we could ask, which *structural* elements are hindering us, for example, as Eliza has been urging, and which are helping us? What changes need to be made to correct the problems we are seeing? And so on for each of the quadrants. This approach can be applied to issues in business as well, of course.

"And how about the levels of relation?" Dot continued. "When we discussed them yesterday, it seemed that you from the Hill thought they applied to you in Congress. Do you still think that?"

"We were just discussing that during the break," Dexter said. "We talked about how some relationships in society are simply set up to be at lower levels of relation—relationships between competing sports teams, for example, between opposing lawyers, and so on. Some of our systems produce *breaking* and *blocking* by design. And they are supposed to. Not every situation invites convergence. The whole point of a football game, for example, would be lost if the opposing players tried to move together to compounding. Within the same team, of course, but not with the opposing team; that's not how the game is designed. Similarly, the rights of defendants in our legal justice system wouldn't necessarily be advanced if their lawyers were building compounding relationships with the prosecutors who are trying to put them in jail. Originally, we were thinking that Congress might be more like these cases, where lower levels of relation are to be expected simply by design."

"But you don't think that now?" Dot asked.

"No. And Arlo put his finger on why. It's because we *aren't* like sports teams or lawyers whose stakeholders are in competition. Whether Democrat or Republican, we are elected by the same team—the citizens within our areas. Whether people voted for us or not, we are supposed to represent *all* of them. Which means, then, that we work for the same team and that the levels of relation between us are therefore critically important for the good of the electorate, so that we can *make water* on their behalf."

"Hmm, interesting," Dot said. "That sounds right to me. So, if members of Congress should be striving for higher levels of relation together, that would give us a way to plan and measure progress across the quadrants, wouldn't it? The guiding question could be: *What realities in each quadrant are hindering and helping productive relation?*"

"Yes, that makes sense," Arlo said.

"What else that we've talked about might be useful when considering our politics?" Dot asked.

"The relational maps," Sam replied. "We could build one for the House and another for the Senate."

"We could also build the societal relational maps that we talked about yesterday," Dexter said. "The combination of all those maps would give us a good picture of where things stand relationally in Congress and across society. We could then tackle the lower relational nodes and work on raising them."

"But how?" Sam asked. "What could we do to work on raising them?"

"That's the key question, isn't it, Sam?" Dot said. "What else have we discussed that might guide us?"

He thought about it for a moment. "Maybe the *breaking* and *blocking* discussion," he replied.

"Yes, great," Dot said. "Based on the chart we looked at yesterday, we know what behaviors we shouldn't and should be engaging in across those nodes, from *breaking* at the *division* level of relation up to *bridging* at the *multiplication* level. And what if, from there, you want to *expand* and get to the *compounding* level? What have we learned that could help us with *that*?"

"*Buber*," Zane said. "Offering our *du*."

"Yes. So, let's put these elements together."

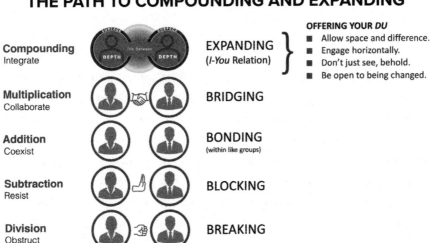

THE PATH TO COMPOUNDING AND EXPANDING

The group looked at the diagram, which now was packed with so much meaning.

"That's really helpful," Dexter said. "It helps me to remember how the various things we've been thinking about fit together. And it gives a bit of a road map for how to begin helping to lift relation."

"Have we covered anything else that might help us in the political realm—or in any other realm, for that matter?" Dot asked.

"Reversing Hegel's Spiral," Jorn answered. "We can make efforts to *start with synthesis.*"

"Excellent, Jorn, thank you. You've really latched onto that, haven't you? That's wonderful. So, individually and collectively, we have lots we can begin working on, don't we?" Dot said.

"What I'm hearing from you is that you want to keep working together to continue helping each other apply what we have been learning. We can discuss and decide whether we want to take on political issues as part of that. If so, great. If not, we can focus on those issues with the team from Congress. But before we work out the details of how we will continue our work together, I want to point out something that I think has great significance.

"Do you remember yesterday when Ricardo was sharing with us how we can expand, both individually and as groups?"

People around the room nodded.

"One way to keep pointing in the direction of growth relationally is to think of what I sometimes call *the next We.* In our personal lives, we grow as our concerns expand to include more people. One question I can ask myself to keep growing is, *Whose perspectives and experiences am I not currently considering?* As I expand my care and concern to include them, I grow into my *next We.* I grow from caring about me, to caring about people who are like me, to caring about people who are unlike me, to caring about people who don't like me, and so on.

"The process at the group level is the same. Wherever you find yourself at any given moment, growth is always in the direction of *the next We.* That's the core truth that has distinguished human beings from every other life form on this planet: We have been able, in fits and starts, to expand the experience of ourselves to include more other selves, and to grow our groups to include additional and different groups. These convergences have fueled innovations that no individuals or separate groups could have pulled off on their own. More than any other factor, the possibility of this kind of *relational leap* is what has set human beings apart.

"That's the work we've continued here together, at a time in our history when we are turning away from that core historical lesson. Referring to the history Arlo has shared with us regarding the Constitutional Convention, are we up to the challenge today? If we had been delegates to that convention, would we have ended up with a country? Would we have beheld and considered each other enough to hold tightly to each other while we grappled with our differences?

"After these two days together, as I look around at all of you in this room, and having experienced what we experienced together, I can say, with confidence, *yes*! I believe you *would* have been up to the challenge of that day. And for that reason, I believe you are up to the challenge of this day as well.

"The country *needs* you to be up to that challenge. We need to be up to that challenge together.

"More than ever, in our homes, our businesses, and our politics, we need, as Arlo has reminded us, *a more perfect Union*."

26

A New Beginning

Zane hung back while the group members said their goodbyes to Dot. When the last of them had left the room, they were alone.

She looked at him with a kind smile.

It wasn't lost on Zane that a room he would have avoided at all costs just two days earlier was a space he didn't want to leave.

"I'd like another chance," he said.

"At what?" Dot asked.

"At a *next We*. I don't think we ever became that over the years we worked together. And that's on *me*."

"Didn't you learn anything here?" She laughed. "It's on *us*."

"Well, *I* am part of *us*."

"Yes, and *I* am part of *you*, Zane. To understand relation is to understand that you, me, and all the other people in our lives and organizations are not static, separate things but bundles of relation—bundles of relation relating to and influencing each other. We're more like verbs than nouns, events rather than things. Every encounter changes the dynamic of who we are. And, interestingly, of who we *have* been. Don't our own histories feel different to us now than they did two days ago?"

Zane thought about it. "Yes, they actually do!" he said in surprise.

"Relation changes the meaning of everything," Dot said. "Including the past. It's what makes us and remakes us. It's quite a remarkable thing, isn't it?"

"Yes." Zane nodded. "It is."

"It's been good to see you, Zane. And you've got this."

"I'm glad at least one of us has that kind of confidence in me anymore," he said with a melancholic chuckle.

"I didn't mean you *singular*; I meant you *plural*. If you remember that, you've got this."

He nodded.

"There's something I need to tell you," she said. "From something you said earlier, it seems you've heard that I recommended your promotion to the Bellweather executive team over your father's opposition."

"Yeah, I know about that."

"But it isn't true, Zane. Your father was never opposed to your promotion."

"What do you mean? He told me so himself."

"That was just his tough dad act. He didn't want you to be disadvantaged by people thinking you were just riding his coattails. Or by you believing that either. So, he never let on to how highly he thought of you, probably even to you. He didn't *come up* with the idea of promoting you to the executive team—he never would have done that for the same reason—but he wasn't opposed to the move, believe me. He was so proud of you, Zane."

Zane felt himself starting to tear up again.

"Frank had a shell, like all of us. But I've never known someone who was so tender to the core. As he gave me more and more responsibility after I returned to the company, I spent a lot of late nights in the office wondering if I was up to the task. Seeing my office light still on, he would

A NEW BEGINNING

drop by, just to see how I was doing. And he would just listen. I never felt an agenda pressing against me, nor a judgment. He just let me unfold.

"Anything good that I've done in the years since then has been due, in part, to those conversations. I discovered myself through your dad, Zane. I became who I am through the back-and-forth of our dialogue—our conversations, our reactions to each other, our putting our heads together to solve hard problems. There is no way I could have led Bellweather without what he put into me, and there is no way I'd be prepared to do what I'm doing now had he not helped to open a *between* where he and I could become more than either of us alone could have ever been.

"One of my favorite Martin Buber quotes is when he said, 'Many . . . acquire relations which they do not make real, that is, which they do not use to open themselves to another; they squander the most precious, irreplaceable, and irrecoverable material; they pass their life by.'[46]

"Your father, Zane, did not squander his life. He learned how to open himself to growth by making his relations real."

"But he wasn't so great at expressing affection, or even approval, to his kids," Zane said.

"No, he wasn't. If he had a do-over, I bet that might look a bit different."

Zane thought about his relationships with Jackson and Allison, and with Laney. *I'm not so good at that either*, he thought.

A new thought and desire flashed into his mind: It wasn't enough just to call his kids. He needed to join them. The kinds of discussions he'd been avoiding with them shouldn't happen over the phone. He knew how easy it was for him to stay behind his pane of glass on a phone call. He needed to get to an airport.

"It's fortunate that you and I still have do-overs, isn't it?" Dot asked.

He nodded. "Yeah, it is."

They smiled at each other, and Zane suddenly felt filled by something that was hard for him to name. *This must be Buber's "leaping fire,"* he thought.

"Okay, Zane, have a safe drive home," Dot said, as she turned to leave.

"Wait!" he called out.

She turned to him again.

"You'll help us, won't you?" he asked. "At Bellweather?"

Dot paused and looked at the floor for a moment.

When she looked back up at Zane, he saw something he'd never seen in her before, just as he'd never seen it in his father. Dot had tears in her eyes.

"Yes, Zane. I'll help you."

EPILOGUE

You might be wondering what happened next in the story. Did Zane hop on a plane and go see his kids? Did he and Laney become friends again? Did he continue to engage with Dot, and did they work on issues at Bellweather together? If so, what impact did that have on the company? Were Zane and Rita able to raise their levels of relation? Did Cree keep his job? Was the Bellweather team able to revamp their leadership program as Rita was recommending? And what happened in Congress, or with the team at PERC?

One can forget something central to the book's message when reading the story, and that is that the characters you are reading and wondering about have not been separate from you. After all, *you* have been the one finding meaning in their journeys. Your reading of this book, like every other part of your life, has been a relational experience, and what's real is not Zane or any of the other characters but rather what has been coming up for you as you have been relating with them. Your desire to know what happens next for them is, in one way or another, a desire to know what will happen next for you.

So, what *will* happen next for you? *You* will be the author of that story. Will you approach life from a relational perspective from here forward? What will that look like? Will you create a relational map of your organization and see what becomes possible as you raise your levels of relation? Will you work on your own relational leadership skills and empower the people around you to do the same? Will you work on extending your *du* more intentionally and authentically to others? Will you endeavor to become a *Bridger* and *Expander* in your personal and professional circles and community? Will you commit yourself to *starting with synthesis*? In a world that is breaking apart, your answers to these questions may be the very efforts that will help your own teams, organizations, and communities to pull together.

Speaking of pulling together, you and I have been engaged in a relational conversation across time and space while you have been reading this book. And many other readers and leaders have launched on the same relational journey. The transition from a *thing-based* to a *relational* view of the world is not easy. From experience, I've learned that it helps to work on it together, just as the group in the book chose to do, and as Zane and Dot decided to do as well.

If you are interested in personal help, organizational help, or in opportunities to become a relational change-agent—my colleagues and I have prepared ways you can join with us and others on the same leadership journey the Glenstone group has begun. On the chance you, your team, your organization, or your community might be interested, I share some ideas and opportunities in the section at the end of the book entitled "What's Next?" (page 246).

In the meantime, I'll be cheering you on as you write the next chapters of this story.

And as you join with others across divides to make water.

ACKNOWLEDGMENTS

I give special thanks to all those who read early versions of *You and We* and offered invaluable critiques and insights.

My partner Kathrin Peters's multiple readings and suggestions shaped the book in profound and countless ways. There is literally not a single page in the book that wasn't dramatically improved by her collaborative efforts and insights. I would have listed her as a co-author had she allowed it.

Chad Ford offered detailed feedback that pointed me toward simpler and more compelling ways to convey some of the book's more challenging ideas. Those of you who might have been turned off by overly complex scientific explorations owe Chad a big thank-you!

Bruce Berger was among the earliest readers whose enthusiastic feedback let me know that I was on the right track. I reached out to him frequently for feedback, and his lightning-fast but thoughtful responses were invariably helpful.

Greg Bullard's honest, unvarnished feedback led to many substantive changes in the manuscript. Among those were changes that made Frank Savage a much more likable and relatable character.

Anthony Clark's thoughts and insights led, among other things, to the inclusion in the book of a very interesting story from his own life.

ACKNOWLEDGMENTS

Alex Alton's feedback resulted, among other improvements, in a more interesting and nuanced discussion of Seurat's painting in chapter 5.

Andrea Hoban strongly encouraged me to include an epilogue, which is a feature you can now thank her for!

I also want to thank Yaïsa Gottenbos for her helpful feedback and insights from a European reader's perspective, and Adel Al-Saleh, Mark Ferguson, Anna Yardley, Colten Yardley, Sarah Ebert, Gabe Rosen, Tony Barr, Sarah Bain, Brian Blaha, Jason Carson, and many others for their helpful feedback and encouragement at key times during the writing process.

I also want to thank the Withiii Leadership clients whose relational efforts to reshape their organizations and leadership efforts have been so inspirational and instructive to me. Your willingness to open yourselves to leading, organizing, planning, and executing in entirely new ways gave birth to this book in ways you don't realize.

Thank you as well to all who weighed in with opinions online regarding title options and cover designs. At times, I felt like arriving at the right title was as heavy a lift as writing the book! We considered hundreds of options, but you never tired of my requests for more feedback. I love where we landed, and we never would have arrived there had you not shared your opinions so generously.

Finally, I thank the outstanding team at BenBella Books and the whole Matt Holt imprint team—Matt Holt, Katie Dickman, Lydia Choi, Brigid Pearson, Mallory Hyde, Kerri Stebbins, Jessika Rieck, and Ariel Jewett. Thank you for your early belief in the book and its message and for your enthusiastic execution of the project. It has been a delight working with you every step of the way.

NOTES

FRONT MATTER

1. Born in Austria, Martin Buber was a German philosopher whose most famous book, *I and Thou*, elucidates the inherently relational nature of human existence. This particular quote is found in Martin Buber, *I and Thou*, translated by Ronald Gregor Smith (New York: Charles Scribner's Sons, 1958), 18.

2. Carlo Rovelli is an Italian physicist whose work around quantum gravity is on the cutting edge of modern physics. He is a prolific author and a leading proponent of the relational interpretation of quantum physics. This particular quote is from Carlo Rovelli, *Reality Is Not What It Seems: The Journey to Quantum Gravity*, translated by Simon Carnell and Erica Segre (New York: Riverhead Books, 2016), 135.

3. Pierre Teilhard de Chardin was a French paleontologist and Catholic priest. In both his scientific and religious writings, he wrote powerfully about how matter, life, and thought all progress as differences come together. You can find this particular quote in Pierre Teilhard de Chardin, *The Future of Man*, translated by Norman Denny (New York: Image Books/Doubleday, 2004), 66.

4. After over three million copies had been sold, in 2024, Arbinger replaced *Leadership and Self-Deception* with an entirely different book under the same title (but a new subtitle). I had no involvement in that fourth edition or potential future editions of the book, but I stand firmly behind all prior versions, which have the subtitle *Getting Out of the Box*. Arbinger also produced a new fourth edition of *The Anatomy*

of Peace. Although the editorial changes they made in that version weakened the book in my estimation, it is still more or less the same book as before. The ideas, at least, if not all the powerful elements of the original story, have been preserved.

CHAPTER 3

5. These words are inspired by a work of art by Lawrence Weiner that appears on the wall of the entrance area of the main building complex at Glenstone Museum. I have retained some of the spirit of his words while writing a new verse that connects more fully to the ideas in this book.

CHAPTER 4

6. In earlier drafts of this book, I included a chapter with a more extended discussion of how quantum physics demonstrates the fundamental relationality of reality. If you are interested in reading that early draft, you can access it at youandwe.com/sciencechapter.
7. Werner Heisenberg, *Physics and Philosophy: The Revolution in Modern Science* (New York: Harper & Row, 1958), 58.
8. As of the time of writing, *A Sunday Afternoon on the Island of La Grande Jatte* is held in the collection of the Art Institute of Chicago.

CHAPTER 5

9. In his book *The Ghost in the Machine*, the Hungarian-born British novelist Arthur Koestler coined the term "holon" to capture the reality of parts that are also wholes (and wholes that are made up of parts) and to show that reality is made up of nothing but holons from top to bottom. I prefer the term "weon"—*we* capturing how every whole is comprised of smaller things in relation and *on* communicating that it is also part of something larger.

CHAPTER 6

10. You can read about the details of the double-slit light experiment at youandwe.com/lightexperiment.
11. See Carlo Rovelli, *Helgoland: Making Sense of the Quantum Revolution*, translated by Erica Segre and Simon Carnell (New York: Riverhead Books, 2021), 151; and Carlo Rovelli, *Reality Is Not What It Seems: The*

Journey to Quantum Gravity, translated by Simon Carnell and Erica Segre (New York: Riverhead Books, 2016), 135.

12. William Egginton, *The Rigor of Angels: Borges, Heisenberg, Kant, and the Ultimate Nature of Reality* (New York: Pantheon Books, 2023), 281.

13. Classical computers are built on binary bits of 1s and 0s. By contrast, quantum computers run on Qubits, which are bundles of quantum relational probabilities entangled in relationship.

CHAPTER 7

14. Pierre Teilhard de Chardin, *The Future of Man*, translated by Norman Denny (New York: Image Books/Doubleday, 2004), 66.

15. Pierre Teilhard de Chardin, *The Future of Man*, 64.

16. Pierre Teilhard de Chardin, *The Future of Man*, 64, 66.

CHAPTER 8

17. See, e.g., Martin Buber, *The Knowledge of Man: Selected Essays*, translated by Maurice Friedman and Ronald Gregor Smith (New York: Harper & Row, 1965), 107.

18. Martin Buber, *Between Man and Man*, translated by Gregor Smith (Mansfield Center, CT: Martino Publishing, 2014), 170.

CHAPTER 10

19. Teilhard de Chardin wrote extensively about the inner and outer dimensions of everything in existence, including humankind. Outer developments require commensurate inner development or deepening in order to sustain. He also wrote about how individual units combine into wholes. These insights, when taken together, yield a four-dimensional view of the world. Scholars in various fields have applied these four-dimensional categories in their own ways. One of them, Ken Wilber, is quite well known for his AQAL framework. The particular relational four-dimensional view presented here, while informed by others' work, is my own.

20. See, e.g., the study entitled "A Multi-Lab Test of the Facial Feedback Hypothesis by the Many Smiles Collaboration," authored by Nicholas A. Coles and colleagues. It was published in *Nature Human Behaviour* in October 2022. See also "A Meta-Analysis of the Facial Feedback Literature: Effects of Facial Feedback on Emotional Experience Are Small and

234 NOTES

Variable," authored by Nicholas A. Coles, Jeff T. Larsen, and Heather C. Lench. It was published in *Psychological Bulletin* in 2019.

CHAPTER 11

21. As just one example of this, see Richard C. Schwartz, *No Bad Parts: Healing Trauma and Restoring Wholeness with the Internal Family Systems Model* (Boulder, CO: Sounds True, 2021).

CHAPTER 12

22. See G. W. F. Hegel, *Lectures on the Philosophy of History*, translated by Ruben Alvarado (Aalten, Netherlands: WordBridge, 2011).
23. See Martin Buber, *The Knowledge of Man: Selected Essays*, translated by Maurice Friedman and Ronald Gregor Smith (New York: Harper & Row, 1965), 69.
24. Martin Buber writes about the difference between imposing oneself on others, which is a *dominator* approach, and allowing and helping someone to unfold, which is an *emergent* one. See, e.g., *The Knowledge of Man*, pp. 82–85.

CHAPTER 13

25. See Robert Putnam, *Bowling Alone: The Collapse and Revival of American Community* (New York: Simon & Schuster, 2001). See also Arthur Brooks, *Love Your Enemies: How Decent People Can Save America from the Culture of Contempt* (Northampton, MA: Broadside Books, 2019).
26. George Washington, "Letter to the President of Congress," in *The Records of the Federal Convention of 1787*, ed. Max Farrand, vol. 2 (New Haven, CT: Yale University Press, 1911), 665.

CHAPTER 14

27. See Pierre Teilhard de Chardin, *The Future of Man*, translated by Norman Denny (New York: Image Books/Doubleday, 2004); and Pierre Teilhard de Chardin, *The Phenomenon of Man*, translated by Bernard Wall (New York: Harper & Brothers, 1959).

CHAPTER 16

28. See Martin Buber, *I and Thou*. In his translation of this book, Ronald Gregor Smith translated this second way of being as *I-Thou*. Walter Kaufmann, in his 1970 translation of the book, translated it as *I-You*

NOTES

235

(although he retained *I and Thou* for the book's title). *I-You* feels less distant in modern English, which is closer to Buber's meaning. However, *I-Thou* is technically more correct, as the word *thou*, despite how it sounds today, was actually originally the informal and intimate form of *you* in English. On a related note, Buber credited Ludwig Feuerbach for helping him to consider the *I-You* or *I-Thou* relation. (See *Between Man and Man*, pp. 146–48.) A contemporary of Buber's, Ferdinand Ebner, wrote about being *I-Thou*, although completely independently from Buber. See Ferdinand Ebner, *The Word and the Spiritual Realities: The I and the Thou*, translated by Jacob W. Stendel (Washington, DC: The Catholic University of America Press, 2021).

29. See Kenneth Paul Kramer, *Martin Buber's I and Thou: Practicing Living Dialogue* (Mahwah, NJ: Paulist Press, 2003), 15.

CHAPTER 17

30. Martin Buber, *I and Thou*, translated by Ronald Gregor Smith (New York: Charles Scribner's Sons, 1958), 4. This was the passage I referenced in the Preface that caught me short and made me question my understanding of Buber's work. If one's perceptions, feelings, and thoughts are the realm of *It*, then Buber's *I-You* couldn't equate simply to seeing, feeling, or thinking about others as *people* as opposed to *objects*, which had been my belief to that point. The passage awakened me to the very different distinction that Buber was making in his work.

31. Martin Buber, *I and Thou*, translated by Walter Kaufmann (New York: Simon & Schuster, 1996), 55.

32. The word *thou* used to be the informal form of *you* in English. However, this has been completely lost in modern English, as *thou* now sounds old, formal, and reverential.

33. See Iain McGilchrist, *The Master and His Emissary: The Divided Brain and the Making of the Western World* (New Haven, CT: Yale University Press, 2009); and Iain McGilchrist, *The Matter with Things: Our Brains, Our Delusions, and the Unmaking of the World* (London: Perspectiva Press, 2023).

CHAPTER 19

34. See Kenneth T. Gallagher, *The Philosophy of Gabriel Marcel* (Barakaldo, Spain: Barakaldo Books, 2020), 53.

NOTES

35. See Martin Buber, *The Knowledge of Man*, pp. 75–78. See also Maurice Friedman, *Encounter on the Narrow Ridge: A Life of Martin Buber* (New York: Paragon House, 1993), 362–63.

36. See, e.g., Gabriel Marcel, *Man Against Mass Society*, translated by G. S. Fraser (South Bend, IN: St. Augustine's Press, 2008), 122; and Kenneth T. Gallagher, *The Philosophy of Gabriel Marcel* (Barakaldo, Spain: Barakaldo Books, 2020), 47–56.

37. See Martin Buber, *Between Man and Man*, translated by Gregor Smith (Mansfield Center, CT: Martino Publishing, 2014), 170.

38. See Martin Buber, *The Knowledge of Man: Selected Essays*, translated by Maurice Friedman and Ronald Gregor Smith (New York: Harper & Row, 1965), 72–88.

39. See Martin Buber, *The Knowledge of Man*, 107.

CHAPTER 21

40. See Martin Buber, *The Knowledge of Man*, 21–22.

41. See Martin Buber, *The Knowledge of Man*, 60.

42. Martin Buber, *I and Thou*, translated by Ronald Gregor Smith (New York: Charles Scribner's Sons, 1958), 12.

CHAPTER 22

43. This sculpture, by Jeff Koons, is called *Spit-Rocker*.

CHAPTER 23

44. This sculpture, by Tony Smith, is called *Smug*.

CHAPTER 25

45. See Robert D. Putnam and Shaylyn Romney Garrett, *The Upswing: How America Came Together a Century Ago and How We Can Do It Again* (New York: Simon & Schuster, 2020); and Katherine M. Gehl and Michael E. Porter, *The Politics Industry: How Political Innovation Can Break Partisan Gridlock and Save Our Democracy* (Boston: Harvard Business Review Press, 2020).

CHAPTER 26

46. Martin Buber, *Between Man and Man*, translated by Gregor Smith (Mansfield Center, CT: Martino Publishing, 2014), 170.

INDEX

A
abuse, 98
addition-level relationships
   and bonding behaviors, 110–115,
      121
   in four-quadrant organizational
      analysis, 83–84, 86, 89, 111,
      126
   and levels of relation, 56–59,
      63–66, 70–71, 73, 118, 126,
      214
   in relational maps, 63–66,
      70–71, 73, 214
   and social capital, 109
antithesis, 100–104, 207. *See also*
   Hegel's Spiral
attitude dimension in four-quadrant
   organizational analysis, 54,
   77–84, 86, 126
   and human development, 94–95
   and levels of relation, 109,
      119–121, 126
   surface and depth, 163–164
availability (openness), 104, 163,
   205, 212

B
background and introduction to
   characters in story
   Bellweather Labs, 3–9, 11–15,
      17–20
   conference facilitators, 19, 27
   leadership conference purpose,
      21–22
   members of Congress, 21
   PERC executives, 21
Bathing at Asnières (Seurat), 38
behavior dimension in four-
   quadrant organizational
   analysis
   applied to individuals, 78–79
   and human development, 94–95
   and levels of relation, 54, 109,
      119–121, 126
   and organizational success,
      80–83
   outer dimensions, 78–79
   surface and depth, 163–164
behaviors and activities at relational
   levels, 110–114, 119–120, 121
   109, 126

238   **INDEX**

beholding others, 184–186, 204–206

"being in one's head" *(I-It)*, 137, 141–149, 165, 185, 205–206, 209–210

between relation *(I-You/I-Du)*, 55, 69, 137, 143–148, 156–157, 165–170, 178–180, 182, 184–185. *See also* offering *du*

blocking behaviors, 110–113, 115, 121, 157, 218–219

bonding behaviors, 110–115, 121, 157

boundaries, 91, 170

Bowling Alone (Putnam), 109

breaking behaviors, 110–113, 115, 121, 147, 209, 218–219

breaking open relations, 162–166, 170

bridging behaviors, 110, 112–115, 121, 157, 168, 219

Buber, Martin

the *between*, 55, 69, 144, 148–149, 157, 167–170, 178

"being" people, 164

Buber's Hyphen, 135–139, 141–148, 168

and compounding level of relation, 61. *See also* compounding-level relationships

on dominators injecting "rightness" into others, 102

I-in-itself, 137

I-in-relation, 137

I-It relation, 137, 141–145, 148. See also *I-It* relation (being within one's head)

"image" people, 164

independent opposites, 180–181

interhuman space, 168

I-You relation *(I-Du)*, 137, 143–148, 168, 179–180. *See also* offering *du*

leaping fire concept, 168, 225

opening to others, 61, 225

psychologizing the world, 142, 147

separation as illusion, 134, 137, 139, 141–142

and T. S. Eliot, 180–181

within, 145–146, 148–149

"you," German words for (*sie* and *du*), 145–147

Buber's Hyphen, 135–139, 141–148, 168

C

change

openness to, 167, 185, 204–205

organizational change and use of relational maps, 119. *See also* relational maps

change in essence, 19, 122, 129, 203

closed-off relations, 162–166, 170

collective efforts

and dimensions of organizational analysis, 78–79, 119. *See also* 4-Dimensional Playing Field

and making water analogy, 44–48. *See also* Fourth Law of Relation (we progress by uniting)

minimizing individual efforts and totalitarian leadership, 194–196, 199–200

communication, three dimensions of, 167–168

INDEX

communion, 168

communities
  and bonding behaviors, 111
  and human development, 94
  relational maps for, 75. *See also*
    relational maps
  and social media, 113

community dimension in four-
  quadrant organizational
  analysis
  and culture, 79, 83
  and human development, 94–95
  importance of, 82–83
  inner dimensions, 78–79
  and levels of relation, 84,
    119–120, 126–127

compounding-level relationships
  and boundaries, 170
  breaking and blocking behaviors
    in, 218
  and breaking open, 170
  and Buber's Hyphen, 61,
    135–136, 139, 170, 219. *See*
    also Buber's Hyphen
  and expanding behaviors, 110,
    112–115, 121, 135, 219
  in four-dimensional
    organizational analysis,
    83–84, 170
  and levels of relation, 57, 59, 61,
    63, 118, 126
  and offering *du*, 219. *See also*
    offering *du*
  in relational maps, 63–64, 71,
    73–75
  and relationships, 139, 169–170
  and social capital, 109

compression, convergence, and
  emergence, 47–48, 57, 121–122

connection, signs of, 167–168

Constitutional Convention,
  114–115, 215, 221

convergence, 47–48, 57, 121–122.
  See also compounding-level
  relationships

culture, 79, 83, 158

D

depth interactions, 48, 142–143,
  162–168, 204

Descartes, René, 92, 134–136, 144,
  207–208

differences
  and creating opposition, 97–99
  and dominators versus emergent
    leaders, 120–121. *See also*
    leadership
  and Hegel's Spiral (thesis,
    antithesis, synthesis), 100–
    104. *See also* Hegel's Spiral
  importance of, 96
  in *I-You* relationship, 179, 185, 204
  and making water analogy,
    95–96
  us/them lines, 103

disincentives, 75, 78

division-level relationships
  breaking and blocking behaviors
    in, 110–111, 113, 115, 121,
    219
  in four-dimensional
    organizational analysis,
    78–79, 83–84, 169
  and levels of relation, 56, 59,
    63–64, 118, 126, 169
  in relational maps, 63–64, 71,
    73, 219
  and social capital, 109

240 INDEX

dominator view of leadership,
102–104, 112, 120–121, 127
double-slit light experiment, 41
du, offering. *See* offering *du*

E

e pluribus unum (out of many,
one), 215. *See also* Fourth Law
of Relation (we progress by
uniting); unity
Einstein, Albert, 42
Eliot, T. S., 180
emergence, 47–48, 121–122, 168
emergent view of leadership,
102–104, 120–121, 127
expanding
behaviors, 92–95, 110–115, 121,
135, 219–221
and boundaries, 170
and Buber's Hyphen, 135–136,
139. *See also* Buber's Hyphen
and connection, signs of, 167–169
and emergent leadership,
102–103
and levels of relation, 121, 139,
157, 167, 170. *See also* levels
of relation
offering *du*, 219–220. *See also*
offering *du*
in politics, 113–115
and social media, 113
expansion, 92–95, 102

F

First Law of Relation (everything
you see is relation)
and laws of relation, 31–32, 117
tic-tac-toe analogy, 29–31, 48,
99, 117
4-Dimensional Playing Field

addition-level relationships in
four-quadrant analysis of
organizations, 83–84, 86,
89, 126
compounding-level relationships
in, 83–84
dimensions of, 77–87
division-level relationships in,
83–84
group dimensions, 78
individual dimensions, 78
inner dimensions, 78
lack of accountability example, 79
multiplication-level relationships
in, 83, 86
outer dimensions, 78
political system analysis, 217
subtraction-level relationships in,
83–84
visibility into organizations for
relational mapping, 76
Fourth Law of Relation (we progress
by uniting)
and expansion of lines, 95–96.
See also organizational
divides
and four-quadrant organizational
analysis, 120
and laws of relation, 48
and levels of relation, 118
making water analogy, 45–49,
61, 74, 95–96, 113, 120, 167,
169, 194, 218
relational process, 47–48
Franklin, Benjamin, 114

G

German words for "you" (*sie* and *du*),
145–147. *See also* offering *du*
Gilded Age, 215–216

INDEX

gridlock, 102

H

Hegel, Georg Wilhelm Friedrich, 97–100

Hegel's Spiral (thesis, antithesis, synthesis), 100–104, 120–121, 207, 220

Heisenberg, Werner, 32

horizontal relationships, 182–185, 204–205

human connectedness, 136

I

I-in-relation concept, 137. *See also* Buber, Martin

I-It relation (being within one's head), 137, 141–149, 165, 185, 205–206, 209–210

independent opposites, 180–182

influence audit, 208

interhuman space, 168–169

intersubjective, 168

I/other (mind/world split), 93, 134–136

isolationism, 47

I-Thou relation. See *I-You (I-Du)* relation

I-You (I-Du) relation (the between), 55, 69, 137, 143–148, 156–157, 165–170, 178–180, 182, 184–185. *See also* offering *du*

J

judgment of others, 110, 147, 149, 158, 182, 209

Jung, Carl, 92

K

Kohl, Helmut, 146–147

L

laws of relation. *See also* levels of relation

First Law of Relation (everything you *See* is relation), 29–32, 48, 99, 117

Fourth Law of Relation (we progress by uniting), 45–49, 61, 74, 95–96, 113, 118, 120, 167, 169, 194, 218

Second Law of Relation (everything is built by relation), 32–33, 35–40, 47–48, 117–118, 194

Third Law of Relation (how we interact is who we are), 41–44, 48, 118

leadership
dominator view of, 102–104, 112, 120–121, 127
emergent view of, 102–104, 120–121, 127
and honesty, 106–109
relational approach to, generally, 32, 43–44, 55, 118, 208
totalitarian, 194–196, 199–200

levels of relation. *See also* relational maps; specific levels of relation
and behaviors of breaking, blocking, bonding, bridging, and expanding, 110–115, 121, 135, 157. *See also* specific behaviors
described, 55–59, 71
in family relationships, 125–126
and four quadrants of dimension (behavior, attitude, structure, and community), 110–114, 119–121. *See also* specific quadrants

242   **INDEX**

levels of relation *(continued)*
    and laws of relation, 118
    in political systems, 218
light experiment (light as a particle
    and a wave), 41–42

M
Madison, James, 114
making water analogy, 45–49, 61,
    74, 95–96, 113, 120, 167, 169,
    194, 218
Marcel, Gabriel, 163, 168
McGilchrist, Iain, 149
mind/world split *(I/other)*, 93,
    134–136
multiplication-level relationships
    and bridging behaviors, 110,
        112–115, 121, 157, 168, 219
    in four-dimensional organizational
        analysis, 83, 86
    and levels of relation, 57–59, 71,
        118, 126
    in relational maps, 63–65, 71,
        74–75, 214
    and social capital, 109

N
next We, 220–221, 223

O
offering *du*, 146–148, 165, 177–186,
    195, 204–205, 210, 219, 228
one-up and one-down versus
    horizontal approaches,
    182–183. *See also* horizontal
    relationships
opening to others (availability), 61,
    74, 95, 104, 148, 163, 166–167,
    185, 225

openness to change, 167, 185,
    204–205
opposites, co-created (reactions and
    responses), 99–100
organizational charts, 55, 69
organizational divides. *See also*
    differences
    and expansion of lines, 92–95
    and gridlock, 102
    and importance of differences,
        95–96
    me/not/me line, 91–92
    me/other line, 92–94
    silos, 56–57, 85, 89–90, 111
    us/them lines, 90, 94, 103

P
Paterson, William, 114
persona, 92, 205
pointillism, 33, 39–40
political reform, 215–221
productivity, in four-dimensional
    organizational analysis, 57, 59,
    83
Progressive Era, 216
psychologizing the world, 142, 147,
    156
Putnam, Robert, 109

Q
quantum theory and quantum
    computing, 43, 118

R
Reagan, Ronald, 146
relation
    described, 31–32
    laws of. *See* laws of relation
    versus relationship, 169

INDEX

relational capital (social capital), 109–115

relational charts, 55–56, 69. *See also* relational maps

relational drag, 73, 76

relational field, 69, 170

relational growth, 220–221

relational lift, 73, 76, 220

relational maps
addition-level relationships in, 63–66, 70–71, 73, 214
for communities, 75
compounding-level relationships in, 63–64, 71, 73–75
creating, 61, 63–71, 212–214
division-level relationships in, 63–64, 71, 73
in government, 218–219
multiplication-level relationships in, 63–65, 71, 74–75, 214
purpose of, 119
societal, 219
subtraction-level relationships in, 63–66, 71, 73
for teams or departments, 71–76

relational nodes, 69, 73, 118, 219

relational understanding of reality.
See also specific laws of relation
described, 29
and differences, importance of, 46–47
dual truths of everything being made of parts-in-relation and being part of a larger whole, 39–40. *See also* Second Law of Relation (everything is built by relation)
and existence, 42–43
and leadership, 44, 208

nonrelational space, no existence of, 42–43

process of compression, convergence, and emergence, 47–48, 57, 121–122

and quantum theory, 43, 118

tic-tac-toe analogy, 29–30

relational view, 69. *See also* relational maps

relationship versus relation, 169

remote work, 48

responsibility, 196, 198, 208–209

Rovelli, Carlo, 42

S

Second Law of Relation (everything is built by relation)
and laws of relation, 40, 48, 117–118
Seurat's painting analogy, 32–33, 35–40, 48, 117–118, 194

seeming versus *being*, 164–165

Seurat, Georges, 32–33, 35–40, 118, 194

Sherman, Roger, 114

The Silmarillion (Tolkien), 174

silos, 56–57, 85, 89–90, 111. *See also* organizational divides

social capital (relational capital), 109–115

social media, 110, 113, 164

space
independent opposites (allowing differences), 179–182, 209
the *between* (interhuman), 55, 69, 119, 167–169, 184–185, 204–205. See also *I-You (I-Du)* relation
and relation in science, 42

space *(continued)*
    and status of parties (horizontal versus one-up or one-down positions), 182–184, 204–205
status and offering *du*, 182–185, 204–205
structure dimension in four-quadrant organizational analysis
    and bridging behaviors, 115
    and human development, 94–95
    importance of, 81–83
    and levels of relation, 86, 119–120, 126–127
    as outer dimension, 78–79
subtraction-level relationships
    and blocking behaviors, 110–113, 115, 121
    in four-dimensional organizational analysis, 83–84
    and levels of relation, 56, 59, 118, 126
    in relational maps, 63–66, 71, 73
    and social capital, 109
A Sunday Afternoon on the Island of La Grande Jatte (Seurat), 33, 35–40, 118, 194
surface interactions, 162–166
synthesis, 100–104, 207, 220. *See also* Hegel's Spiral

T

Teilhard de Chardin, Pierre, 47–48, 57, 121–122

thesis, antithesis, synthesis (Hegel's Spiral), 100–104, 120–121, 207, 220
Third Law of Relation (how we interact is who we are), 43–44, 118
    light experiment analogy, 41–42, 48
tic-tac-toe analogy (everything you see is relation), 29–31, 48, 99, 117
Tolkien, J. R. R., 174
Twain, Mark, 215–216

U

unity, 48, 120, 215. *See also* Fourth Law of Relation (we progress by uniting)

W

Washington, George, 115
water as combination of hydrogen and oxygen, 45–49. *See also* making water analogy
within one's head (*I-It* relation), 137, 141–149, 165, 185, 205–206, 209–210

Y

"you," German words for (*sie* and *du*), 145–147. *See also* offering *du*

ABOUT THE AUTHOR

Jim Ferrell is the founder of Withiii Leadership, a company devoted to helping individuals and organizations apply and operationalize the relational insights introduced in *You and We*. Prior to founding Withiii, Jim was a longtime managing partner of the Arbinger Institute. He has written a number of bestselling books, including the original versions of the international bestsellers *Leadership and Self-Deception* and *The Anatomy of Peace*, with millions of copies in print and each ranking among the all-time bestsellers in their respective categories.

Over his nearly three decades working with corporate and governmental leaders, Jim has developed a reputation as one of the world's great innovators in the areas of leadership, culture change, conflict resolution, communication, and interpersonal connection. He has a unique ability to grasp complex ideas and translate them into elegantly clear models and applications. He is a regularly featured speaker at trade and corporate conferences and has mentored leaders and trained workforces of many of the most well-known organizations and brands in the world.

Jim has degrees in economics and philosophy and is a graduate of Yale Law School. For years he taught a law school course on the topic of overcoming divides. He is the recipient of multiple awards on peacebuilding.

Jim is originally from Seattle and currently resides in the Washington, DC, area. He is an avid cyclist and a longtime but decidedly average golfer. You can connect with Jim through the contact form on his company's website at Withiii.com, by signing up for Withiii's newsletter on all things related to connectivity and relational leadership, or by following him online.

WHAT'S NEXT?

I founded Withiii Leadership to help individuals and organizations learn, apply, and operationalize the relational ideas introduced in this book. This means that if you are interested, you don't need to tackle your story alone; we can work on these issues together. We have created a portal at YouAndWe.com to provide resources and help. On this portal, you will not only find bonus chapters to the book and a chance to get in touch with me about your experience, but you will also discover various resources and ideas to help you do any or all of the following:

- Continue to learn and grow on this path.
- Learn to "extend your *du*" more effectively and often.
- Practice relational leadership in both your professional and private life.
- Learn to apply what I call the "Seven Rules of Relation," which are areas of practice that build upon the ideas in *You and We*.
- Engage with others who have embarked on the same relational leadership journey.
- Implement and utilize tools and resources to help you grow and keep these ideas front and center.
- Access four-dimensional, relational data on your organization, just as the organizations in the book received about theirs.
- Get 360-degree feedback about your relational leadership abilities.
- Empower your leadership team or organization to raise your collective relational scores and efforts and to operationalize these ideas across your group or company.
- Partner with me and my colleagues in this effort, anywhere around the world.

If you're up for it, I'd love to continue our stories together. Join me and other fellow travelers at YouAndWe.com or at Withiii.com. I look forward to connecting with you there!

YouAndWe.com
Your portal for what's next